Yale French Studies

NUMBER 133

"Detecting" Patrick Modiano: New Perspectives

SPECIAL EDITORS: RICHARD J. GOLSAN AND LYNN A. HIGGINS

D1551717

Yale French Studies

Richard J. Golsan and Lynn A. Higgins
  Special editors for this issue
Alyson Waters, *Managing editor*
Editorial board: Maurice Samuels (Chair),
  R. Howard Bloch, Morgane Cadieu, Jennifer Carr,
  Tom Connolly, Edwin Duval, Jill Jarvis, Laura B.
  Jensen, Alice Kaplan, Christopher L. Miller,
  Pierre Saint-Amand
Assistant editor: Robyn G. Pront
Editorial office: 82-90 Wall Street, Room 308
Mailing address: P.O. Box 208251, New Haven,
  Connecticut 06520-8251
Sales and subscription office:
Yale University Press, P.O. Box 209040
New Haven, Connecticut 06520-9040

Designed by James J. Johnson and set in Trump
  Medieval Roman by Newgen North America.
  Printed in the United States of America.

ISSN 044-0078
ISBN for this issue 978-0-300-22889-2

RICHARD J. GOLSAN AND
LYNN A. HIGGINS

Editors' Preface: New Perspectives on Patrick Modiano

In his speech accepting the 2014 Nobel Prize for Literature, Patrick Modiano (b. 1945) remarked that he had the impression of having written each novel as a continuation of the previous one, like one long work that somehow, outside his awareness, eventually added up to an *oeuvre*. Elsewhere, he often repeats that he feels he has written the same novel over and over. Yet his loyal readers and fans eagerly anticipate the almost annual "new Modiano." They have avidly followed the slow but distinct evolution of his work and appreciated the variations from book to book that seem subtle but that utterly distinguish one novel from all the others. An impressive body of critical writings has risen to the challenge of opening new windows onto this writing that seems "limpid" and straightforward but that continues to elude categorization and to fascinate critics and casual readers alike.

Major international recognition such as that conferred by the Nobel Prize meant, in the United States at least, that a writer known by few outside of academia has suddenly become widely acclaimed and perhaps even canonical, despite the reactions of early skeptics who questioned whether he deserved the Prize. Commercial as well as academic presses have rushed into print numerous translations, and whereas in the past few of his novels were available in English, now almost all of his work is. The same was true of Modiano's illustrious French Nobel laureate predecessors: Claude Simon, J. M. G. Le Clézio, even Albert Camus and Jean-Paul Sartre (who declined the prize and became all the more notorious for it). That being said, what place Modiano will ultimately hold in the pantheon of "great French writers," at least for Anglophone readers, remains to be seen.

YFS 133, *"Detecting" Patrick Modiano*, ed. Golsan and Higgins, © 2018 by Yale University.

Modiano appears to be continuing along his established path, however, undeterred by glory.[1] We believe that his "Nobel moment" is nevertheless a propitious juncture for reassessment and overview, for new questions and new angles of vision. But given the apparent "sameness" or "repetitiveness" of his work, as well as the substantial amount of academic criticism devoted to him over the years, is there anything new to say about him? As the contributions to this issue of *Yale French Studies* make clear, the answer is a resounding "yes" (although Modiano himself would probably prefer a subtler adjective than "resounding").

Some of the contributors to this volume of essays place the writer in a variety of new, broad contexts, from literary and cinematic traditions such as Surrealism and *film noir*, to Jewish humor, and classical tragedy. Others focus on specific novels or groups of novels in order to listen in on Modiano's dialogue with other writers, such as Le Clézio and the Hussards. Still other essays confront the writer of fiction with his own implicit historiographic tendencies. And two contributors examine Modiano's fascination with names and places.

Other contributors reexamine some of the enduring themes of the Modiano universe: the Dark Years, memory and loss, Modiano's *roman familial*, and so on. They also grapple with the paradoxes that have characterized the author's work from the beginning. For example, Maryline Heck examines the troubled relations between Modiano and Serge Klarsfeld in order to probe tensions between the worldview of a novelist and that of a historian. Richard Golsan sheds new light on ways the layers of Modiano's obsession with the past negotiate connections and disconnections between family memory and the history of the Occupation. Bruno Blanckeman takes on the thorny question of how Modiano's writing encompasses both classical narrative and Modernist form.

Examining Modiano's interactions with and debts to the right-wing Hussard writers, Marc Dambre opens new perspectives on Modiano's early literary relations as well as influences. Exploring Modiano's lifelong engagement with the cinema, Lynn Higgins looks into the

---

1. He worried briefly that the Nobel Prize might paralyze him—and indeed, he had not published a book since just before the Nobel announcement. However, the fall of 2017 has seen publication of both a new novel (*Souvenirs dormants*) and a play (*Nos débuts dans la vie*). He wrote the play first, he says, to jumpstart his writing. See Nelly Kaprièlian, "Comme des mauvais rêves qui reviennent," interview with Patrick Modiano in *Les inrockuptibles* 1142 (18–24 October, 2017), 10.

possible significance of the author's claim that he has memories from before his birth. For Van Kelly, juxtaposing Modiano's *Voyage de noces* with Le Clézio's *Étoile errante* clarifies the historical and political perspectives of both authors. Gerald Prince delves into the evocative richness of Modiano's nouns, proper and otherwise, in *Rue des boutiques obscures*, and Susan Suleiman explores Jewish humor and its links to Jewish identity in Modiano's only truly humorous novel, *La place de l'étoile*. While Modiano's attachment to Paris has been widely discussed, Vanessa Doriott Anderson shifts our attention to consider his urban mythologies surrounding another city, Bordeaux.

The editors would like to express their gratitude to a number of people and Institutions that have helped make this issue of *Yale French Studies* possible. Several of the essays published here were originally presented at Columbia University's *Maison Française* in October 2015. We would like to thank the Director, Shanny Peer, for organizing the event and also the French Cultural Services in New York for their support. We would also like to thank the translators of the essays by Blanckemann, Dambre, and Heck—Ellen Collier, Mary Claire Chao, and Christina Lord respectively—and Van Kelly, for helping us locate such able translators. We would also like to acknowledge Alyson Waters, the Managing Editor of *Yale French Studies*, with whom it is always a pleasure to work! Richard Golsan would like to thank the France/Texas A&M University Institute (*Centre d'Excellence*), the French Consulate in Houston, and most especially Sylvie Christophe, the Cultural Attaché there, who has been a wonderful colleague and friend. Lynn Higgins is grateful to the Dartmouth Dean of the Faculty Office and the Leslie Humanities Center for their encouragement and support.

BRUNO BLANCKEMAN

Patrick Modiano or Writing as *Nocturne*

From the moment of his literary debut, author Patrick Modiano has collected prize after prize, with the regularity of a metronome: the Roger Nimier Prize for *La place de l'étoile*,[1] the Académie Française's Grand prix du roman for *Les boulevards de ceinture* ,[2] the Prix Goncourt for *Rue des boutiques obscures*,[3] the Académie Française's Grand prix de littérature Paul Morand in 2000, the Cino Del Duca World Prize in 2010, the Nobel Prize for Literature in 2014, as well as many more honors and distinctions of lesser prestige. This seemingly endless distribution of laurels does, however, mask a certain irony when situated within the author's own itinerary, which he recounts freely, telling how, as a young student, he preferred the freedom of playing the truant to that of the attentive pupil in the classroom. For half a century, however, a blaze of glory seems to follow a man who has become a celebrity *in absentia*—a man of the shadows, all the more present in the public's mind as he is absent in the media. Between the man and his work, the same paradox exists: how does such a writer of the shadows become a figure who attracts so much light? How does the invisible, hidden side of things overcome obscurity and become perceptible in its own right?

Modiano's oeuvre is a *nocturne*. Clearly playing with the different semantic nuances of this motif, certain novels even illustrate it with their own ambiguity, using a hint of confusion that affects the use of the simplest language, even that which is most immediately clear:

1. Patrick Modiano, *La place de l'étoile* (Paris: Gallimard, 1968).
2. Modiano, *Les boulevards de ceinture* (Paris: Gallimard, 1972).
3. Modiano, *Rue des boutiques obscure* (Paris: Gallimard, 1978).

YFS 133, *"Detecting" Patrick Modiano,* ed. Golsan and Higgins, © 2018 by Yale University.

La ronde de nuit[4] (a race, a cycle, but also a Rembrandt painting), *Rue des boutiques obscures* (an urban setting, a topographical indication, a Roman space, but also an itinerary, an image, an enigma), *Accident nocturne*[5] (trivial expression or dramatic fact), *L'herbe des nuits*[6] (what grass? which nights?). These motifs echo other titles, written too with the black ink of melancholy, reshaping and transposing an intimate distribution of loss and perdition: *Villa triste, Quartier perdu, Dans le café de la jeunesse perdue, Pour que tu ne te perdes pas dans le quartier.*[7] Shadow is as diffuse as the shadows are abundant and all-powerful in Modiano's work—they form an army of specters, those vanished without a trace, anonymous people from old directories, people tortured in the camps, the brother and the father whose errant souls reach out and grab the living. Such a body of work continues to fascinate its audience after half a century because those shadows implicate us directly: shadows divided, his shadows and our shadows, shadows ourselves, sucked into a nether world in which the writer plays the ferryman and his writing the vehicle. They are in harmony with a history that outlines the contours of our own contemporaneity.

Whose contemporaries are we? That is one of many questions that this *oeuvre*, haunted by History and possessed by memory, seeks to answer. Each novel is characterized by its particular darkness—History, the abuses and crimes of war, an originary pain doubled by the torment of childhood memories and their darkness, shadowy recesses that exert a seductive power of some sort of *sinister* beauty, of some maleficent order, upon the characters. The writing itself, and its lunar genius, guarantees the full effectiveness of narratives painted in chiaroscuro. All is clear and yet all remains a blur in the stories they reveal, tales that are retrieved from the depths of consciousness, carried along by a language snatched up quickly and violently from within itself. This *melancholic* writing creates rhythm out of loss and harmony out of lack—absence is its acoustic depth, mourning its chosen melody. This writing both charms and disquiets its readers,

4. Modiano, *La ronde de nuit* (Paris: Gallimard, 1969).
5. Modiano, *Accident nocturne* (Paris: Gallimard, 2003).
6. Modiano, *L'herbe des nuits* (Paris: Gallimard, 2012).
7. Modiano, *Villa triste* (Paris: Gallimard, 1975); *Quartier perdu* (Paris: Gallimard, 1984); *Dans le café de la jeunesse* (Paris: Gallimard, 2008); *Pour que tu ne perdes pas dans le quartier* (Paris: Gallimard, 2014).

placing them into the novel's story, seeming to mask the story itself, in the same position that its characters find themselves faced with their own lives: on the threshold that separates memory from forgetfulness (take as examples some of Modiano's lesser-known works that have not yet attained cult status: *Vestiaire de l'enfance* and *Un cirque passe*.[8])

All mythologies concern origins. The founding legend of Modiano's work hides an undeniable truth, joining a declaration of birth to the end of a world: 1945, the year of the author's birth, the end of World War II. Like a benevolent fairy perched above the cradle, an army of shadows emanates out of the Paris Occupation—one part inherited guilt—and the camps of deportees—one part inherited victimhood. The first part is of the blood—the biographical figure of the father, a black-market trafficker, compromised and ubiquitous within Modiano's first novels. The second is of the heart—the emblematic figure of Dora Bruder and all the rest of the unknown dead within the camps. But the heart is drained of its blood . . . the fault-ridden father is also the father of pain, the shameful Jew who, having betrayed his own, must in his turn pay the price of humiliation, narrowly escaping arrest—the man for whom, as is revealed in *Un pedigree*,[9] his son would seek to have justice restored by writing his first book. The culpable and the innocent, the perpetrator and the victim, the executioner and the one persecuted are inseparable. The unique staging that the first novels develop, each in its own way, takes form via a symbolic appropriation of the facts of both our collective history—the war—and familial history—the father. To experience oneself (in all senses of the verb) as guilty from infancy, like the son of some injurious epoch formed from the rubble, yet rendered innocent by that very birth—such is the literary formula applied in Modiano's first three novels: *La place de l'étoile, La ronde de nuit,*[10] *Les boulevards de ceinture*. It proclaims and exposes the decrepitude of a world guided by chaos, in which all ideological positions are reversible. Simultaneously tragic and buffoonish, as lyrically refined as it is carnivalesque, the narrative, nevertheless, submits to its referent: it destabilizes perspective in favor of open expressionism, bringing logic under the guise

8. Modiano, *Vestiaire de l'enfance* (Paris: Gallimard, 1989); *Un cirque passe* (Paris: Gallimard, 1992).
9. Modiano, *Un pedigree* (Paris: Gallimard, 2005).
10. Modiano, *La ronde de nuit* (Paris: Gallimard, 1969).

of the grotesque and twisting all consciousness into the smirking face of nightmares. Within the collaborator, a resistance fighter cowers, inside of whom another collaborator is crouched, brooding over yet another resistance fighter . . . The fictional situation in *La ronde de nuit*, itself inspired by yet another novel, *Les épées* written by Roger Nimier and published in 1948,[11] appears in the film *Lacombe Lucien* (1974), co-written with Louis Malle.

Starting with *Villa triste*, the shadows slip back into obscurity, having scandalized a nation persuaded that France had never been divided, but was always a singular, solid, *resistant* body, a general's kepi resting on its head, a hammer and a sickle in its hands. From this point on, Patrick Modiano has written from a blind spot. The shadow out of the corner of your eye is the projection of another soul, perceived only in its absence. It is from this perspective, in the shade of the dark years [*les années noires*], that Modiano conceives his many novels, each a finely-tuned modulation to a crucial scene: the throes of history, seeping out of the troubled recesses of collective memory, in the half-sentient stupor of amnesia. The Occupation becomes the literary metaphor of a greater subconscious, haunted for having committed an offense made all the more impossible to expiate by its players' ignorance of their guilt, who believe themselves to be the inheritors, not the perpetrators, of the crime. The fathers' indignity engenders the torment of the sons (exemplified in *Une jeunesse*[12]). These gently rendered readings of pain, delicate, soundless sobs [*sanglots*] à la Paul Verlaine, move the reader's heart. But have we given sufficient attention to the acts of *Resistance* manifest in these texts? To resist forgetting is to write from the deepest recesses of one's emotions, to reposition oneself at square one, to relive them all over again. Whereas Proust creates a circular narrative structure, Modiano's is dislocated around an abyss in time, one that wanders astray, as distinct from Claude Simon's, which is ostentatiously imposed. The narrative swims backward in time through a chaotic realm of disordered dates, independently infiltrating each other over the decades—more numerous from one novel to the next—for characters who are aging in real-time with the author. From the present moment of writing to a point of no return, the same decade seems always to jam the time machine, blocking the hands of the clock (a recurring theme in the

11. Roger Nimier, *Les épées* (Paris: Gallimard, 1948).
12. Modiano, *Une jeunesse* (Paris: Gallimard, 1985).

novels): the 1940s. To resist forgetting thus means undermining it, acting as a partisan of memory as much as its artisan: refining its details where they nest in memory, lusterless residues of the past—memory's piecemeal leavings—making an inventory of the buildings, of the businesses, of the cafés, telescoping the practice of novelists past to evoke Stendhal and his traveling mirror, and that of contemporary historians—think of Ginzburg's microhistory.[13] The indexical model created by the historian as a mode of access to knowledge—inferring from a body of precise details the ensemble that they allow us to reconstitute—finds a testing ground in the detective novel, the genre that sometimes inspires Modiano. Minimalist art, *arte povera*, *ars memoriae*: Modiano's poetics evolves from an initial expressionism to a diffuse impressionism, marking, even to this day, his literary voice. On the heels of a *danse macabre*, maximalism follows a minimalist writing that struggles with its ghostly characters, a *white writing* that evokes effacement through ellipsis, silence through syncope. In this mimetic art of forgetting, tormented still by the glimmer of memory, music—the measure and rhythm of words in the sentence, the pauses printed out as blanks on the page—haunts the soul. This creates a subzone of the text and its meaning which remains subliminal to the narrative and our consciousness. The titles themselves are like a musical partition: *Quartier perdu, Dans le café de la jeunesse perdue, Pour que tu ne te perdes pas dans le quartier* . . . This music, deprived of meaning, creates a subtle charm, a poetic *carmen* that acts on readers, makes them understand, as an accompaniment to the story being told, what it cannot express clearly, but that resonates in the round of its words and reverberates throughout their echo chamber: the millstone of official silence, of a nation's *omertà*, the self-censorship of families, the desiccated voices of the dead that still resound within city walls, the muffled sob of a child who grew up deprived of his youth. Like Duras's *petite musique*, Modiano's creates an infra-logical line of fiction, underlying the novel's economy.

To this art of crafting novels corresponds the posture of the writer who figures fully in the national, and henceforth international, realm from which Patrick Modiano now benefits: to become witness to a world that he did not know. A paradoxical witness who founds his stories not upon a strictly eyewitness account, as in law, but rather

---

13. Carlo Ginzburg, *Mythes, emblèmes, traces: morphologie de l'histoire* (Paris: Flammarion, 1989).

upon a more visionary experience. Such power reveals itself not to be the gift of some extra-sensory awareness, but instead the result of an infra-lucid predisposition. The writer is by profession a man of imagination, as Modiano explains in *Dora Bruder*, and his systematic use of that faculty makes him hypersensitive to the perception of certain parallel situations, to the capturing of certain occult events, even before the clear zones of consciousness perceive them and understand them with any intelligibility.[14] This explanation is certainly a discourse of humility: it refuses to stoop to the caricatured grandiloquence of the seer on duty . . . It *is* nonetheless necessary to grant him the same seriousness that the author does. Over time, as the direct, legal eyewitnesses disappear, the secondary witnesses take over. Although they did not live through the events themselves, they nonetheless remember, without pretending to be historians. If writing, for Modiano, is never a duty of memory, in the commemorative sense of the expression, then it depends on an *ethos* of memory. This role of paradoxical witness has conferred on Modiano's work a magnetic novelistic power as well as a cultural resonance that, above and beyond the success of his works, explains the importance his writing has accrued over the decades.

This positioning is indebted to the distant legacies of Romanticism and Surrealism. In *Dora Bruder*, Modiano pays homage to the Victor Hugo of *Les Misérables*, in whose footsteps he unknowingly places his own, winding through the streets of the same Parisian *quartier*, and also to Robert Desnos, from whose first novel Modiano admits to having unwittingly borrowed the title. Several of the novels remind us, too, of André Breton, wandering, halfway between dream and reality, through nocturnal Paris, haunted by the women of the shadows and genies of the night. The space of Modiano's novels is open to the surreal: a place of vestiges that conserves, like a depot of time, the shattered remains from which his characters are bound to an improbable task of archeological reconstruction. Their literary wanderings materialize the mental comings and goings of a conscience/consciousness [*conscience*] shifting from some worrisome, literally pre/*occupied* present towards an enigmatic past from which some little piece is lacking, keeping it from ever feeling whole (*Remise de peine*[15]), always another "good enough" reason to explain

14. Modiano, *Dora Bruder* (Paris: Gallimard, 1997), 53.
15. Modiano, *Remise de peine (Paris: Gallimard, 1988)*.

away the prejudice that has impacted them (*Pour que tu ne te perdes pas dans le quartier*). Modiano seems also to add a measure of objective chance to the wanderings of his antiheroes, lost in life and losers in history. They evolve, to evoke Breton once again, between *faits-glissades*—gliding through events that do not concern them— and *faits-précipices*—situations that stop them and swallow them whole, a part of their existence being risked without their even knowing why. The equation presented by Breton in *Nadja*—I am whoever haunts me—seems here to take the place of real identity. This unconventional dimension added to the stories results in a progressive see-sawing from the mundane, true-to-life narratives—correlated to districts of Paris, nearby suburbs, or easily identifiable French provinces—toward a parallel universe, disfigured by the fears and the fantasies of a conscience that is disoriented and losing contact. Thus the narrator of *L'horizon*, obsessed with "the dozens and dozens of phantoms" that form, "like in astronomy," a "dark matter . . . more vast than the visible parts of your life," glowing, "scintillating" like "stardust."[16]

But this dual oscillation between dimensions of space-time as a measurement of the world *other* than that of rational experience and as a measure of the author's characters outside of the sole realm of consciousness, goes beyond a purely literary game. It says something about the capacity of an *oeuvre* to resonate with its own era, as well as to summon it forth and even anticipate it. The full historical scope of such work is measured through the eye of this paradoxical witness, inhabited from the very beginning by the author. *La place de l'étoile* appeared one year before *Le chagrin et la pitié* (1969), the documentary in which Marcel Ophuls returns to the phenomenon of Collaboration in the French provinces, and several years before the publication, in English and later in French, of Robert Paxton's work on Vichy France.[17] In 1968, the national decorum, with an aftertaste of censorship, insisted on not speaking about Vichy and of relegating the Collaboration to the lower depths of a murky history, far from the official, gilded national memory, which identified itself only with the Resistance. The first few novels of Modiano, who builds

16. Modiano, *L'horizon* (Paris: Gallimard, 2010), 12; 19.
17. Robert Paxton, *Vichy France: Old Guard and New Order, 1940–1944* (New York: Columbia University Press, 2001).

his barricades with eyes fixed on the past and not on the halcyon, postwar days, *les lendemains qui chantent* of other young people of his generation, crash into the national mythos like a hurled paving stone. In the decades that followed, Modiano's work would develop while, little by little, the long imposed silence around the deportation of Europe's Jews would end after the initial accounts like Robert Anteleme's *L'espèce humaine*[18] were disseminated. *Holocaust*, a Marvin Chomsky miniseries with international acclaim (1979), and *Shoah*, an iconic film by Claude Lanzmann (1985), would each mark in its own way the return of a subject that had become taboo. It is not a question of deifying Modiano's work, but neither should subsequent cultural developments make it seem banal. Modiano's work was pioneering in redirecting national attention back toward Vichy and then toward public recognition of the deportation of Jews. *Dora Bruder* marks the height of a movement that started as a radical provocation, and then as a minimalist writing of identities lost. *Dora Bruder* restores a precise civilian identity to the work's narration, but suspends it in the indecision that affects a character about whom we know nothing at all, aside from the fact she led a fugitive life and died, another unidentified person amongst a mass of nameless deportees. Fiction is thus reinvigorated, and with it the capacity of literature to work from a place of forgetting, to conceive of ways to transmit history in an era where its importance for culture is being relativized.

To take the measure of a body of work is thus to understand its reach, to put into perspective the vision that it proposes of history and the prevailing relationship between that same history and the society in which the novels are published. During the 1970s, novelistic *vision* writing—fiction that conjures, rather than tells, the story of the Occupation—was aimed at contesting political dialogue that had long created an atmosphere of *occultation*, held by men who had belonged to the Resistance, according to whom Vichy could not represent the French state, but rather its counterfeit. From the 1980's to the 1990's, this *vision* writing remained opposed to an ideology of *revisionism* (or negationism) that would punctuate the powerful return of an extreme-right in France, marginalized since the end of the Algerian War. Literary witnessing is what contributes, on the

18. Robert Antelme, *L'espèce humaine* (Paris: La Cité Universelle, 1947).

one hand, to reestablishing an accurate recollection of facts and, on the other, to denouncing their criminal usurpation. Modiano's work invents a narrative form that, articulating a particular relationship with history, gives it a meaning in its own way with the words of tales and of dreams, even if they are those of a muted nightmare. At first ahead of historical research, these novels later crossed paths with those historians who were working on a past that seems impossible to move past, to borrow Henry Rousso's words.[19] This state of resurgence establishes itself from within a system of historicity that historian François Hartog calls "presentism" [*le présentisme*], a measure of time brought back to the absolute present, a distended period of hauntedness endlessly actualizing the past, blocking any possibility of a future.[20] The same is true for Pierre Nora's *Lieux de mémoire*,[21] for its cartography of urban spaces endowed with a memorializing function, and for Serge Klarsfeld and his *Mémorial des enfants juifs déportés de France* (1994) for the name and the person of Dora Bruder, both intersecting with Modiano. An old companionship that evokes others, as when in the nineteenth century the novel and history rubbed elbows to invent a philosophy of history, with Hugo, Michelet, and Jules Verne. Of their common vision, inasmuch as it invents a mythology and a progressive ideology of history, Modiano's work constitutes a repudiation, the end of a relationship with the absolute that had endowed—under the guise of idealism—History, society and its powerful civility, family as the hearth of love, with so many values inherited from the Age of Enlightenment. Modiano's melancholy is an inspiration that opposes this romantic euphoria's momentum. It is the expression of disenchantment with all consciousness of history, at the end of a century that witnessed the multiplication of great combined and collective griefs, wars, and organized totalitarianisms. Thus the teleological space proper to a particular modernity has given way to a spectral dimension that manifests itself in many works from the end of the twentieth century and the beginning of the twenty-first. Antoine Volodine's post-exoticism invents a nihilistic version of this shift: his parallel universe is populated with creatures part

19. Eric Conan and Henry Rousso, *Vichy: Un passé qui ne passe pas* (Paris: Fayard, 1994).

20. François Hartog, *Régimes d'historicité. Présentisme et experiences du temps* (Paris: Éditions du Seuil, 2002).

21. *Les lieux de mémoire*, ed. Pierre Nora (Paris: Gallimard, 1984–1992).

human and part animal who survive in a futuristic setting that never stops living the catastrophe, with its detention camps, its betrayed revolutions, and its system of concentration camps.[22] Michel Houellebecq, for his part, composes in *Les particules élémentaires* a more decadent version, marked by a vision of history in which all living force, all progress intersect via optical illusion with a killing force, a regression.[23] As for Modiano, he develops a melancholic version within novels of aftereffect where scenes both historical and intimate gather their negative charge.

In the author's work, family is presented as a miniature society mimicking, at the personal level, the tremors of History. The mother plays the role of the executioner, by default: actress, she is always absent, even when she is right there. The father plays a role in both camps: that of the executioner, denouncing his teenage son to the police—an episode recounted many times over—and that of the victim, never fully recovered from being taken for nothing more than a wandering Jew. The younger brother, Rudy, has no role: he is the victim, dead at ten, the other "Bruder" from whom the author borrows his birth year and with whom he identifies during the first decade of his life as a writer. Solitude in the family apartment, the mother's little dog that throws itself from the window for lack of attention, always being dropped off with other people; the mother's indistinct women friends when she goes on tour, the boarding school, running away, trafficking old books: this collection of childhood pains and of adolescent revolts, constitutes the intimate repertory of his fiction. And the author rewrites it unflaggingly. From *Les boulevards de ceinture* to *Pour que tu ne te perdes pas dans le quartier*, the adult characters of the novels are summoned by their past and their early childhood. These novels outline the return of the repressed: everything within them is narrated from the voice, and filtered through the point of view, of a child who has lost his way in an adult universe where he seeks to return to the troubled waters of his childhood.[24]

For five decades, Modiano's oeuvre has fashioned a tight ensemble of biographical material in which authentically lived facts are enveloped by their successive variants and surpassed by their many

22. Antoine Volodine, *Terminus radieux* (Paris: Éditions du Seuil, 2014).
23. Michel Houllebecq, *Les particules élémentaires* (Paris: Flammarion, 1998).
24. See Bruno Blanckeman, "Nimier dans le rétroviseur (*La place de l'étoile*)," in *Cahier de l'Herne "Roger Nimier,"* ed. Marc Dambre (Paris: Éditions de l'Herne, 2012).

extensions. It reveals an incessant working-through, throughout which the author reinvents, if not his childhood, at least his relationship to it, and through it, his relationship to history. Thus this cynical fascination with murky figures, double agents, and suspicious characters of the Occupation, which caused him to be read by former Vichy writers (among whom Paul Morand) as a new-generation *Hussar*, has given way to the compassionate empathy felt for the victims. And the victims are always so twice over: during their lives because they were crushed by one of History's aberrations; and after their deaths because they are subsumed into the category of "victim," which dispossesses them of any other individual identity. Dora Bruder is the very image of this double obscurity, induced by the absence of archives capable of chronicling her youth—except for two attempts to run away which would indirectly bring about the Bruder family's arrest—and repeated by her incorporation into the list of Jewish children who were deported and died. The book turns around this double absence in its refusal to amplify Dora by giving her, as in *Voyage de noces*,[25] a substitute literary identity. As the end of the book suggests, only her secret can reveal her, by default, like a gesture of independence addressed to a society unworthy of her words. The ethical and aesthetic power of the work comes from this singular art of perseveration [*rémanence*] *La rémanence* is what persists when all else has been erased, it is the phenomenon that leaves only fleeting tracks in its wake, it is the event of which only a distant echo lingers, already partially unidentifiable. *Rémanent* writing is writing that lets erasure shape its very structures, play with its crumbling paragraphs, erase its frame, fragment its phrases, jot hastily-made notations to the detriment of their narrative coherence. It is narrative decomposition, in sync with the chaos of consciousness/consciences. But with each new work, a story is nevertheless seized at the point where it resists its own erasure; at the point where narrative wages battle against the shadows that would bury it. It is a demand for clarity and the ability to hold the line against its own evanescence.

As an epigraph to *Pour que tu ne te perdes pas dans le quartier*, Modiano chose a quote from Stendhal: "I cannot produce the reality of facts, I can only present their *shadow.*" In Modiano's work, would Plato and the myth of the cave dispute Freud within novelistic

25. Modiano, *Voyages de noces* (Paris: Gallimard, 1990).

narratives as limpid as allegories, like in a *camera obscura* whose chiaroscuro universe of characters, moving about as though disoriented by their own existence, seems a capricious projection? A strange perspective indeed. From one version to the next, Modiano's work centers around a vanishing point, opened up by a crisis situation, that always finds its resolution in a place prior to its own experience in the limbo of existence.

—Translated from the French by Ellen Collier

MARYLINE HECK

Modiano, Klarsfeld, and Dora:
Revisiting a Misunderstanding

Upon the publication of *Dora Bruder*, Serge Klarsfeld expressed his "irritation" about being completely erased from the storyline. It was Klarsfeld who discovered the most important documents and information concerning Dora Bruder and significantly helped the writer during his investigation. Indeed, in a letter to Modiano where he acknowledges receipt of the book, Klarsfeld writes:

> Allow me to note, however, that the investigation, as you recount it, seems more fiction than reality, seeing as I am not mentioned at all. Still, God knows that I worked on finding and assembling the information about Dora before passing it on to you. I do not know if this disappearance [. . .] implies that I was too present in the research stage or if the literary process allows for the author to be the stand-alone demiurge.[1]

Klarsfeld's surprise is understandable since Modiano had lauded him so enthusiastically in an article published in *Libération* in 1994, where he expressed his desire to emulate Klarsfeld's *Mémorial de la deportation des Juifs de France* in his own writing:

> I admired Serge Klarsfeld and his wife Beate who have fought for over ten years to keep the past alive. I am grateful to this man for having forced me and others to experience one of the most shocking discoveries of our lifetimes. [. . .] I tried to follow Serge Klarsfeld's example. While consulting his memorial for days on end—this list of first and last names—I tried to find additional details, an address, the smallest indication about the life of one person or another.

---

1. Published letter in *Patrick Modiano*, ed. Raphaëlle Guidée and Maryline Heck (Paris: L'Herne, 2012), 186. Translated from the French by the translator. Unless otherwise indicated, all translated text is by the translator.

YFS 133, *"Detecting" Patrick Modiano*, ed. Golsan and Higgins, © 2018 by Yale University.

That is exactly what he undertook with Dora Bruder once he discovered her missing person notice in an old newspaper from 1941.

However, the book does depart from Klarsfeld's perspective, most notably because Modiano does not seek to be exhaustive. He does not show all of his cards, including the work completed by Serge Klarsfeld, whom Modiano does not mention. According to Klarsfeld, Modiano may have taken too much artistic license. This is what his letter implies—a letter that will signal, as one might suspect, the end of the two men's correspondence—when Klarsfeld evokes "a *literary* process [that] allows for the author to be the stand-alone demiurge" or the fact that "the investigation, as you recount it, seems more like *fiction* than reality." In other words, for Klarsfeld, Modiano fell victim to what we might call his "Gallimard superego." This superego would have prompted him to create a "literary" work whereas the historian would have expected a more thorough and informative text.

This disagreement raises important questions surrounding the ethical practices of memorial writing. Klarsfeld does not seem to be in a position to understand that Modiano's undeniable "literary temptation" in *Dora Bruder* does not necessarily contradict the memorial project but, rather, gives it structure. If Klarsfeld did not understand Modiano's intent, it is because Modiano distances himself from conventional models such as memorial museums or historical or commemorative writing in the vein of Klarsfeld's *Mémorial*. Now I will discuss what distinguishes Modiano from these models in order to better define his unique work and examine its ethical scope.

MODIANO'S "GALLIMARD SUPEREGO"?

Certain aspects of Modiano's book can appear to be attacks on the truth that a memorial endeavor would seem to require. As Alan Morris notably demonstrated, Modiano did not disclose everything, nor did he provide all of the documents and information in his possession.[2] These silences and approximations might be surprising coming from a narrator/author who otherwise recounts at length not only his efforts as an investigator but also the results of such efforts. Modiano's approach thus clearly differs from that of a historian. He

2. See Alan Morris's article, "'Avec Klarsfeld, contre l'oubli:' Patrick Modiano's Dora Bruder," *Journal of European Studies* 36 (September 2006): 269–93.

regularly emphasizes his refusal or hesitation to pursue the investigation further: "One day I shall go to Sevran." "Someday, I shall go back to Vienna, a city I haven't seen for over thirty years. Perhaps I shall find Ernest Bruder's birth certificate."[3] This hesitation suggests that, although he expressed a desire to follow Klarsfeld in his article in *Libération*, Modiano ultimately chooses an exclusively literary path for himself, drawing inspiration from Robert Desnos, Maurice Sachs, Antonin Artaud, and Jean Genet. Literary references abound, while the social sciences are completely absent. Here, Modiano demonstrates once again his ability to swim against the tide of literary fashion, his contemporaries often preferring to dialogue with the social sciences.

It seems, then, that a deviation from the initial project took place over the course of the book's development. "Literature" seems to have regained the upper hand and, in the end, *Dora Bruder* resembles Modiano's novels more than it does Klarsfeld's *Mémorial*. Even though the writer had already given free rein to his fictional inspiration while writing the novel *Voyage de noces* (1990), based on the same missing person notice, *Dora Bruder* nevertheless closely resembles Modiano's novels. For example, the book is narrated in the first person by a narrator who, this time, is not satisfied with appearing to be an author but who *is* the author. Other elements of his novels include: a narrative schema that adopts that of a police investigation (and more accurately, an unsuccessful investigation), nebulous characters shrouded in a cloud of uncertainty, and the emergence of autobiographical motifs (the runaway [the *fugue*], the figure of the father, and so on). Even the aporetic conclusion indicates a Modiano novel, with a denouement that does not resolve anything. In this regard, it is significant that Modiano did not indicate the genre on the cover of *Dora Bruder*, suggesting the ambiguity that surrounds its literary categorization. Indeed, while *Dora Bruder* is Modiano's only work that comes close to a historical approach, the writer seems to be, in the end, a rather poor historian.[4] In fact, in an interview at the time of the book's release, Modiano states:

3. Patrick Modiano, *Dora Bruder*, trans. Joanna Kilmartin (Oakland, CA: University of California Press, 1999), 14 and 16. Page references throughout will be from this translated edition and will be indicated within the text.

4. This is also the opinion of Nicolas Xanthos, who examines the opposition between Modiano's discourse and that of a historian in his article "Un sentiment de vacance et d'éternité: *Dora Bruder* contre l'histoire," *MNL* 27/4 (September 2012).

For years I have been trying [. . .] to write a biography, a report, to investigate a real fact . . . [In *Dora Bruder*], I came as close as I had ever
been to writing a non-novel. But with so many gaps in the storyline, I
was forced to embellish, to water down the truth. I would like to have
a case file like lawyers do, full of police reports, witness statements,
experts' conclusions. That way, I would no longer need to fictionalize.[5]

Does this obligation of having to "water down" and "fictionalize"
stem from his desire to create a literary work? And even if we set
aside his desire to create a story—and Klarsfeld's *Mémorial* is precisely not a story, because it remains in the elementary and factual
form of a list—do the ethics of memorial writing require holding onto
raw facts? Is Modiano subsequently the victim (or culprit, rather) of
his "Gallimard superego"? Such is the point of view of Klarsfeld, who
criticizes him, in short, for not following his own example. Or, to
put it in Jaussian terms—borrowing H.R. Jauss's notion of a "horizon
of expectations" developed in *Toward an Aesthetic of Reception*—
the lawyer Klarsfeld could not appreciate the originality of what the
writer Modiano was proposing in *Dora Bruder* because he remained
focused on his usual "horizon of expectations." As it happens, there
is a double horizon: the "Gallimard horizon of expectations" (the one
he attributes to Modiano) and his own "*Mémorial* horizon" (the one
he criticizes Modiano for not applying). It seems that Klarsfeld could
not see that *Dora Bruder* is a text that refuses to borrow from other
possible approaches. Instead, the text asserts itself as a unique interpretation of memorial writing—including individual responsibility—
in the face of the tragedies of History.

MEMORY WORK AND A DESIRE TO INVESTIGATE

It is possible to interpret Modiano's decision to omit certain information or documents about Dora differently. Modiano certainly expresses regret in his book that he did not have more documents and
first-hand accounts to feed his investigation. He laments that the head
of the boarding school Saint-Cœur-de-Marie, where Dora resided, died
in 1985, three years before he knew about the young girl's existence.
However, he quickly adds: "But, after all, what could she have told
me? A few humdrum facts of daily existence" (35)? This question

5. Olivia de Lamberterie and Michel Palmiéri, "Patrick Modiano dans la peau
d'une femme," *Elle* (8 February 1999) : 71.

suggests that the gathering of information is not everything. It is also important to note that these "documentary" traces are collected, in large part, at the beginning of the book. The narrator reveals the information he has acquired and lays out the documents in his possession. But these documents are written in a cold, bureaucratic language that does not seem particularly informative to him. In fact, this is not where he truly captures the essence of Dora, but rather later in the book, when he walks around Paris and "feels" her presence or, in this case, her absence.

The trace of Dora and those who, like her, were left behind is actually the absence of a trace, a "hollow trace," modeled on the emptiness that defines these missing people above all else from this point forward. It is by finding this trace, rather than collecting documents, that the narrator is able to discern something of them, and that their memory is finally revealed to him:

> It is said that premises retain some stamp, however faint, of their previous inhabitants. Stamp: an imprint, hollow or in relief. Hollow, I should say, in the case of Ernest and Cécile Bruder, of Dora. I felt a sense of absence, of emptiness, whenever I found myself in a place where they have lived. (21)

To turn the absence of a trace into a critical trace is to multiply the potential marks of Dora and other missing people, possibly present in all the places where they lived. Then, as the text continues, there are the places where they did not live that, although not empty, feel empty to the narrator. At the very end of the text, he states:

> I walk through empty streets. For me, they are always empty, even at dusk, during the rush hour, when the crowds are hurrying toward the entrances of the métro. I think of her in spite of myself, sensing an echo of her presence in this neighborhood or that. The other evening, it was near the Gare du Nord. (119)

Conceptualizing the trace as "hollow" allows Modiano to carry out two types of reconstruction. The first is that of a gap, or absence, since the lack of physical traces left by the Bruder family paradoxically makes possible the proliferation of virtual traces. The second is a reconstruction of the story itself. *Dora Bruder* is far from being "embellished" or "watered down," as Modiano evoked in his interview.[6]

---

6. Although, we might attribute these comments to the author's strong tendency toward self-deprecation.

Simply filling in the gaps is not the only justification for resorting to fiction. It is more a question of *carrying out* memory work, to give it shape within and through the writing process. These traces of Dora only exist because Modiano writes them; the trace is tied to its enunciation, suggesting a performative form of narrative discourse.

Thus, a paradoxical relationship between Modiano and his documents materializes in *Dora Bruder*. On the one hand, it is possible that the document retains a particular aura (as with the missing person notice), acting as a medium for imagination. On the other, its effectiveness as a medium for memory seems questionable. In the book, the document cannot stand alone, and it lacks eloquence. By itself, it is unable to reflect the memories of the departed. However, by not revealing certain things, by sometimes leaving clues unresolved instead of pushing the investigation through to the end, perhaps Modiano is suggesting that he does not want to bring his investigation to a close. This refusal to conclude, as Raphaëlle Guidée argues, serves to "neither repeat Dora's annihilation, nor definitively close the investigation, which recalls her brief existence and preserves the emotions surrounding her disappearance." For Guidée,

> the partial transcription of sources from which the narrator rediscovers snippets of the young girl's story speaks not so much to the methodical research based on clues and evidence as it does to the intense desire to remember [*désir de mémoire*], and the dubious nature of an investigation of individuals whom no one in the present necessarily remembers.[7]

Modiano keeps the investigation open, maintaining his desire to investigate even beyond the end of the book. Guidée's remarks strike me as crucial for understanding what is at stake in *Dora Bruder*. It allows us to consider from another angle what seemed, in Klarsfeld's eyes, to infringe upon the memorial project: the fact that Modiano refuses to reveal all the results of the investigation has as much importance as the story's unfolding.

Modiano does not speak about himself in an attempt to take center stage, but as a way to give life to Dora's memory. It is in this context that we must understand Modiano's insistence on his ability to

7. Guidée, "L'écriture contemporaine de la violence extrême: à propos d'un malentendu entre littérature et historiographie," *Histoire et littérature en débats*, available under "Colloques en ligne" on the *Fabula* website: http://www.fabula.org/colloques/document2086.php. Consulted 12 October 2015.

wait, which returns as a leitmotiv in the text.[8] It is also a question of understanding the ethos, tinged with romanticism, that the writer builds over the course of the book. One can imagine that this ethos is what irritated Klarsfeld, who must have worked just as patiently as Modiano. What Serge Klarsfeld saw as Modiano's distorting reality to his own advantage should instead be understood as his way of expressing Dora's trace within him, the way she dwells in his memory, and how the permeation of the trace within him fuels his desire.[9]

This desire can also be understood in the way Dora feeds Modiano's imagination. Fictionalizing her was another way for Modiano to pursue this desire to investigate—which he literally confirms within the text when he alludes to the writing of *Voyage de noces*: "In the novel I had written at a time when I knew almost nothing about Dora Bruder, *I wanted to keep her in the forefront of my mind*, so the girl of her age whom I called Ingrid hides in the Free Zone with her boyfriend" (60, emphasis added). These moments of fictional writing are reconfigured and are heavily invested in the memorial project.

We understand this when Modiano mentions "imaginative leaps" (42) belonging to the work of writers, or even the "gift for clairvoyance" (42) as being affiliated with a writer's trade. He firmly anchors his work in a literary rather than a historical tradition (with hints of Rimbaud, as it so happens). About half-way through the book, the structure departs from administrative documents and other information gathered about Dora, with the mention of his "gift of clairvoyance" and then finishes with examples of said "gift." This structure leads one to believe that Modiano gives as much importance to these experiences, part fantasy, part hallucination, as to the accumulation of objective facts. In fact, one can talk about quasi-hallucinatory experience in certain passages, such as the one where Modiano says: "Today, I am visited by the memory of a German writer. His name was Friedo Lampe" (76). These experiences come to a climax at the end of the book, with the excerpt that I already cited, when the narrator sees the streets as empty even though it is rush hour.

8. For example: "It took me four years to discover her exact date of birth [. . .] And a further two years to find out her place of birth: Paris 12th arrondissement. But I am a patient man. I can wait for hours in the rain" (10).

9. Klarsfeld himself suggests that Modiano's desire to pursue his investigation of Dora has affinities with amorous desire in his last letter to Modiano: "Perhaps you are in love with Dora or her shadow and, even though we have looked for her together you insist on keeping her for yourself, in making her loved by the reading public."

The literary genealogies in which the writer places himself would be those of Romanticism, Rimbaud, and Surrealism (the latter because of its coincidences and its urban *dérives*). In other words, these are not the most obvious authors or movements associated with memorial writing. The reading of Modiano's text is made all the more difficult because it is situated within a framework outside of historical writing, and because it is contrary to what Modiano had affirmed in his 1994 article on Klarsfeld's *Mémorial*. *Dora Bruder* was misunderstood precisely because it is situated far from institutionalized, memorial initiatives. Yet Modiano was writing exactly at the time when memory was institutionalized, as François Hartog emphasizes in *Régimes d'historicité*. According to Hartog, everything begins in the 1980s, which "experienced the unfurling of a great wave—that of memory. With its alter ego, more visible and tangible—patrimony, which was to protect, to categorize, to value, but also to rethink. They erected memorials, renovated and multiplied museums, big and small."[10] This "great wave of memory" gave birth to the "museums of memory" that were in full flower at the time Modiano was writing. While his investigation was taking place, The United States Holocaust Memorial Museum opened in Washington D.C. in 1993, which is exemplary of these new museum projects.

MODIANO: DISTANCING HIMSELF FROM OFFICIAL MEMORY

The experience of memory that Modiano proposes in his book differs from and even opposes what these museums offer, relying as they do on the accumulation of documents, data, photographs, and artifacts. Informational documents and photographs are placed next to clothes, shoes, and other objects that belonged to camp prisoners. It is of primary importance for museum designers that objects be *real*, that they form an authentic trace of the past. In the Washington D.C. museum, visitors can enter an actual railroad car that transported prisoners, or go into an Auschwitz barracks. The museum's organization encourages a form of document sacralization designed to give the visitor access to the past by means of its authenticity. As Hartog explains: "The exhibit combines photos, films and objects, like so many

10. François Hartog, *Régimes d'historicité: Présentisme et expérience du temps* (Paris: Seuil, coll. "Points," 2012 [2003]), 25.

strategies meant to grasp the real. Indeed, the museum's organizers
thought it was important to have authentic objects, present in their
materiality, which would allow for an almost physical connection."[11]
The museographical plan thus rests on a different understanding of
documents from the one that Modiano implements in *Dora Bruder*;
in the museum, the documents are considered "stand-alone," leading visitors to a form of *reenactment*, giving them the possibility to
replay, in some way, something from this past. Hartog explains: "The
museum's pedagogy aims to lead visitors during their visit to iden-
tify with the victims. Beyond placing the Holocaust in a museum
for centuries to come, the visit aspires to transform each visitor, and
they count in the millions, into a representative witness, a substitute
witness, a *vicarious witness*."[12]

The "memory work" of museums thus differs from what Modiano
develops in his book, which questions the ability of documents to give
us access to the past under the pretext that they are authentic and au-
thenticated. The writer proposes another form of memory work [*faire
œuvre de mémoire*] that is eminently subjective and cannot be au-
thenticated, but that consists of feeling/seeing (the verbs vary) the
traces of Dora over the course of her urban wanderings, through certain feelings of emptiness, certain resonating effects or magnetism.
Modiano proposes a concept of the trace that is eminently subjective
and immaterial, which distances itself from monuments, slabs of memorial stone, or commemorative sites. One could contrast Modiano's
"trivial" places of congested intersections and empty streets where
he feels Dora's presence with the "monumental" museum, whose
very architecture was designed, from beginning to end, to signify,
symbolize, and provoke emotion. The Washington D.C. museum
structures the experience of memory as a guided tour, from the architecture of the building to the distribution of victims' personal records
at the entrance, which invites each visitor to take on the story of a
deportee. One can then contrast this *obligation* to remember [*devoir
de mémoire*], with what better corresponds to Modiano's writing: a
desire to remember [*désir de mémoire*].

The writer's refusal to accept the monument, his way of making
the work of memory essentially intimate and immaterial, is also a

11. Hartog, "Le témoin et l'historien," *Gradhiva* 27 (2000): 1–14. http://www
.oslo2000.uio.no/program/papers/m3a/m3a-hartog.pdf
    12. Ibid.

refusal of the spectacle—this spectacle that is the Holocaust into which others (artists as much as museographers) plunge without a second thought. Modiano refuses facile, effortless emotion, which perhaps explains his choice not to show photographs of Dora. There is a certain modesty about Modiano, which is made explicit on the last page of the book, when the narrator places himself on the side of those who choose to respect the "secret" of Dora's *fugue*.

Dora Bruder is therefore also a book that is written *as an act of opposition*—something the ease and elegance of Modiano's writing has the tendency to make the reader forget. Modiano writes against these models, or at least, at a distance from them: at a distance from historical discourse and against memorial and commemorative institutions. What has not been emphasized enough is how *Dora Bruder* is also a book with a critical agenda. The narratorial ethos, developed over the course of the book between romantic isolation and hostility toward institutions, suggests as much.[13] The narrator's words lend themselves to being understood as words of resistance to the historicization of memory, which would permanently inscribe memory in an enclosed past, that of museumification or of archives that the "sentinels of oblivion" (11), as he calls them, keep closed. Modiano's gesture to incorporate the absence of the other into himself is fundamentally melancholic, but he would define melancholy as resistance, as criticism, as the power to create another ethics of memory.

CONCLUSION

Creating a work of memory while writing at a distance from non-literary models is also, for Modiano, a way of establishing the autonomy of literary writing. If Klarsfeld had been part of the book, his name alone[14] would have reduced this autonomy because it is laden with a certain history and dense symbolism. The fact that the

---

13. In fact, one should take note that Modiano often criticizes authority figures and administrations of all kinds. This is highlighted at the beginning of the text, when Modiano is taking the next step at the *Palais de Justice*: "At first, I took him for one of those sentinels of oblivion whose role is to guard a shameful secret and deny access to anybody seeking to uncover the least trace of a person's existence. [. . .] My hesitation earned me a rebuke from another functionary. Was he a guard? A policeman? Was I supposed to hand over my shoelaces, belt, wallet, as at the gates of a prison?" (11–12).

14. On the other hand, the fact that this name appears in paratexts must be emphasized: Modiano mentioned his debt to Klarsfeld in various interviews. This was undoubtedly what Modiano considered his proper place.

autonomy of literature can constitute its ethical dimension is no longer a paradox since Barthes's reflections on the responsibility of the writer are even more radical—not only about the autonomy but also the autotelism of literary writing.[15] For Modiano, this autonomy that literary discourse has in relation to other discourses that are institutionalized, established, and expected *in fine*, represents a powerful form of criticism in and of itself.

—Translated from the French by Christina Lord

15. For example, Barthes writes in "Authors and Writers" ["*Écrivants et écrivains*"] that "the author is a man who radically absorbs the world's *why* in a *how to write*. And the miracle, so to speak, is that this narcissistic activity has always provoked an interrogation of the world: by enclosing himself in the *how to write*, the author ultimately discovers the open question par excellence: why the world? What is the meaning of things? In short, it is precisely when the author's work becomes its own end that it regains a mediating character: the author conceives of literature as an end, the world restores it to him as a means" [Roland Barthes, *Critical Essays*, trans. Richard Howard (Evanston, IL: Northwestern University Press, 1972), 144–45.

MARC DAMBRE

In the Wake of the *Hussards*, a Young Modiano Writes against the Tide

French universities have long denied the talents of Patrick Modiano, in large part because they resented his "conservative endorsements."[1] These include choosing Jean Cau to write the preface for *La place de l'étoile*, his personal relationship with Paul Morand, his published interview with Emmanuel Berl, and winning the Roger Nimier Prize. Indeed, with the exception of Berl, who for this reason will not be considered here, all of these writers have ties to the French literary movement known as the *Hussards*. Modiano's suspected conservatism and that of this small literary galaxy are therefore on common ground. Paul Morand and Roger Nimier, who developed a close father-son relationship over the years, became the driving force behind *Hussard* politics. Jean Cau, who worked as Sartre's secretary from 1947 to 1956, initially came out in strong opposition to the *Hussards*, but his own political evolution brought him closer to their position by the the early 1960s. The fourth and final member of this literary boys' club is Bernard Frank. Frank inadvertently baptized the group in a controversial article published in a 1952 issue of *Les temps modernes*, but was accused of betrayal the following year. He has since been considered a "left-wing *Hussard*."

The relationships that Modiano fostered with senior *Hussards*, Morand in particular, represent a sort of literary crossroads. Indeed,

1. Jacques Lecarme, "Variations de Modiano (centered on *Accident nocturne*)," *Lectures de Modiano*, ed. Roger-Yves Roche (Nantes: Editions Cécile Defaut, 2009), 20. Regarding literary links between the "Occupation Trilogy" and *Les épées* and *Le Hussard bleu* by Nimier, see *Drieu la Rochelle ou le bal des maudits*, "L'agent double," "Perspectives critiques" (Paris: P.U.F., 2001), 99–127. Unless otherwise noted, all translations from the French in this article are by the translator.

YFS 133, *"Detecting" Patrick Modiano*, ed. Golsan and Higgins, © 2018 by Yale University.

while these relationships were distant, they were clearly not lacking in depth. Parallels and divergences are easy to find when comparing Modiano's writings to those of *Hussards* such as Roger Nimier, Antoine Blondin, Jacques Laurent, and Michel Déon. Moreover, a textual examination reveals similarities between the works of Nimier, Frank, and even Cau, which until now have been neglected or simply ignored. These similarities make it possible to better situate Modiano, with the goal of reinterpreting the early period of his writings, a period that includes *Lacombe Lucien*.

PAUL MORAND, A MASTER FOR *HUSSARDS* ONLY

Patrick Modiano was not an avid reader of Paul Morand. During his adolescence,[2] he considered the elderly writer a "has been" and associated him with Maurice Dekobra, author of *La Madone des sleepings* (1925), a best seller with intellectual and worldly appeal—the opposite of what Morand would have considered a flattering comparison. It was therefore with mixed feelings that Modiano began to read Morand. Shortly before turning twenty, he read Morand's *France-la-doulce*,[3] although he didn't take it seriously. In his mind the book was written ironically. Rereading it later, he found that the xenophobic novel lived up to its dry and anti-Semitic reputation. Generally, Modiano had little esteem for the storyteller, although he did appreciate his descriptions of cities and accounts of his travels, citing the writer's acute sense of observation and stylistic force. Modiano also appreciated Morand's writing on history and literature in *Monplaisir*, his collection of essays published in the late 1960s. That his curiosity and interest remained piqued is evidenced in Morand's *Journal inutile* (2001), wherein Modiano's name is mentioned nearly twenty times.

When Modiano won the Roger Nimier prize in 1968 for *La place de l'étoile*, it was the beginning of a relationship with Morand built on brief personal exchanges and invitations. This relationship was characterized by restraint and silence, as evidenced by the laureate's first meeting with Morand, who was at that time jury chairman. Forty years after the fact, Modiano recalled that Morand "was strangely taciturn. He didn't say a word to me, but he gave me a letter

2. "Paul Morand, un revenant," interview with Michel Crépu, *Revue des deux mondes* (June 2010): 89–93.

3. Patrick Modiano, *Romans*, "Bibliothèque de la Pléiade" (Paris: Gallimard, 2005): 355–448.

relating what he thought of my book. Then, he called three or four times to see me. It was all quite laconic."[4] The burgeoning writer had already met such literary giants as Queneau and Prévert, but it was never his intention to become anyone's disciple. He confirmed as much in his critique of the *Hussards* stating, "I didn't want a tutor and I was always shocked that young writers like Michel Déon and Roger Nimier would go see him like he was a kind of master."[5] Modiano maintained his relationship with Morand until Morand's death in 1976, as evidenced in *Journal inutile*. Meanwhile, the elder supported Modiano's *Les boulevards de ceinture* for the Grand Prix du roman de l'Académie, which the book won in 1972. Fittingly, in 2000 it was Modiano who received the prix Paul Morand awarded by the Académie Française. (Note that Romain Gary refused the award.)

In the spring of 1968, Morand's endorsement of *La place de l'étoile* removed any doubt surrounding his appreciation of Modiano's work. This is also confirmed by his criticism of *La ronde de nuit*: "The novel was lacking—and I only say this out of my affection for you— that smile amidst the suffering, that seductive grace, that charming, carefree juvenility that immediately drew me to you." Thus, while we do not have the letter Morand left on *La place de l'étoile* at our disposal, we do have his reiterated praise a year later.[6] Morand's disappointment highlights his initial esteem and his high expectations. Indeed, his admiration of the quality of Modiano's writing and the expression of his suffering never wavered in *Journal inutile*. As a well-known anti-Semite, Morand's support and the reasons that motivated it are questionable to say the least. Was he conscious of turning a blind eye? Was it paternal fantasy? Fear of tarnishing his legacy? All of the above? These are the terms he uses to describe the Modiano he loves, the one he finds in *Les boulevards de ceinture*:

> Third Modiano. Good. As in Todd's *L'année du crabe*, which, Lacretelle tells me, will get the Goncourt, the young, errant Jew, searches for the father he will never find. A fatherless generation (Blondin, Nourissier, Nimier, etc.) who, after murdering the father, regrets never having had one.[7]

4. Interview with Philippe Lançon, *Libération*, October 4, 2007.
5. "Paul Morand, un revenant," 90.
6. Morand, *Journal inutile, 1968–1972*, vol. 1. November 8, 1969 (Paris: Gallimard, 2001), 291. The September 11, 1969 letter is recopied in the journal entry on this date.
7. Morand, *Journal inutile, 1968–1972*, vol. 1. October 20, 1972 (Paris: Gallimard, 2001), 811.

Morand assimilated Modiano into the generation of *Hussards* that included Blondin and Nimier (with Nourissier on the periphery); being without a son himself, Morand could in this way create a substitute paternity through symbolic filiation. This quest for a son reappears at the end of *Journal*, where Modiano's name is once again associated with the *Hussards*, in particular Nourissier and Nimier.[8]

Morand's creation of this fictitious genealogy clearly suggests some ulterior motives. As for the *Hussards*, they admired Morand's talent. In the 1950s they were even sometimes referred to as *"Morandiens."* Indeed, if Morand established contact with them it was because he considered that they had great potential. Was he hoping to carry on his legacy posthumously? One event points toward this theory. In 1965, during a visit with the young Modiano, Jacques Chardonne suggests that the former take on the project of editing his correspondence with Morand, who had already given his approval. However, the visit with Modiano went poorly and nothing ever came of the suggestion.[9] And yet, Morand had already thought to do something similar with Nimier, banking on his generosity. As a critic and later an advisor to Gaston Gallimard, Nimier worked tirelessly to separate himself from the literary purgatory in which the Vichy regime had stranded him. In referring to *La place de l'étoile*, Morand uses terms such as "grace," "appeal," and "carefree," words that he also used to refer to Nimier, his "son."[10] The situation, while not altogether the same, was not altogether different. Morand showed surprise that Modiano had read his books. Was his surprise sincere, a sign of selfish satisfaction, or an attempt to bring them closer?

If Morand's calculations for posterity and quest for paternity made the author turn a blind eye to the Jewish heritage of this "young, errant Jew [searching] for the father he will never find," it must still be noted that his reference to Olivier Todd cited above only distinguishes categories and not generations. The novelist behind *La place de l'étoile* is openly provocative and freely plays on anti-Semitic feeling. The anti-conformist narrator of the novel, Raphaël Schlemilovitch, goes as far as anti-Zionism. Morand can appreciate a literal reading of the

8. Morand, *Journal inutile,1973–1976*, vo. 2. March 19, 1976 (Paris: Gallimard, 2001), 772.

9. François Dufay, *Le soufre et le moisi. La droite littéraire après 1945. Chardonne, Morand et les hussards* (Paris: Perrin, 2006), 211.

10. Marc Dambre, Presentation, Paul Morand–Roger Nimier, *Correspondance 1950–1962*, (Paris: Gallimard, 2015), 12–13.

text while still acknowledging "that smile amidst the suffering," a semi-masochistic source of good books. As a result of this ambiguous approach, the anti-Semitism might be passed off as phony. The ex-Vichyste Morand is notably absent from *La place de l'étoile*, unlike in the works of Céline, Rebatet, and others. Morand may like to think he is innocent, indeed, he has always thought that; moreover, in reading *Le Figaro littéraire* he discovered Modiano's provocative but troubling declarations about his own anti-Semitic tendencies.[11]

When the young Modiano went to see Jacques Chardonne in the spring of 1965, he knew that the writer had corresponded with Nimier and that this had even inspired his novel *Lettres à Roger Nimier*. However, the appeal of the recently deceased *Hussard* only partially explains this visit. In fact, Modiano wanted to question Chardonne on his collaboration during the war. The sick old man was able to circumvent the conversation, however, and instead sent Modiano away with signed copies of his complete works! Modiano remained particularly frustrated about not obtaining an answer on a topic he found truly scandalous: Chardonne had excluded Jewish poet Heinrich Heine from his *Anthologie de la poésie allemande*, which was published in 1943, citing that his decision was a matter of personal taste. But Modiano would not give up, that is, not entirely. The passage from *La place de l'étoile* on Heine, which includes a quote and translation in the notes, is actually a thinly veiled reference to Chardonne and shows the first traces of Modiano's repressed anger.[12] Thirty years later in Modiano's *Des inconnues*, Chardonne, while not mentioned by name, is clearly identifiable by the title of one of his works that had made its comeback in 1952, *Vivre à Madère*. Chardonne is unmistakable as the "very hard-looking man with thick eyebrows who wore a bow tie" at a book signing.[13] In a moment of extreme, albeit repressed, violence, the author gets scared and starts to sweat. The hero of the novella then lays his hand on the author's shoulder and asks him to sign the book to Alberto Zymbalist. Alberto was the name of Modiano's father.

Even subtler is the fictional, yet equally negative, portrayal of Morand. In *Vestiaire de l'enfance*, several of Morand's characteristics can

11. See Bernard Pivot, "Demi-juif, Patrick Modiano affirme: 'Céline était un véritable écrivain juif,'" *Le Figaro littéraire* (April 29–May 6, 1968): "It's true that at times I am anti-Semitic . . . perhaps it is nostalgia for assimilation."

12. Modiano, *La place de l'étoile* (Paris: Gallimard, Folio 698, 2014), 40–41.

13. Modiano, *Des inconnues* (Paris: Gallimard, Folio 3408, 2000), 90.

be found in the contentious character of the solitary writer: "The secret behind the old immortal's longevity, which spanned the century, must lie in the total absence of that organ that tires so quickly: the *heart.*" Later, when Modiano was asked if Morand's books had made an impression on him, his reply echoed the same sentiment: "Actually, no. He had no *heart.*[14] [. . .] For me, his books inspire no feeling." He refuses to consider Morand to be a "great writer" because of his cold heart.[15] This critique did not prevent him, however, from giving a bit of helpful advice: "[. . .] it should have been limited to include only the best passages. In doing so the book would have resembled Prince de Ligne's *Fragments,* a work that Morand held in high esteem."[16]

THE *HUSSARDS*: "FAMOUS LITERARY CARTOONS"

While attending the prestigious Lycée Henri IV, Modiano advised a close friend of his to read Antoine Blondin, Roger Nimier, and Paul Morand.[17] A curious and voracious reader, Modiano had read these authors because their works focused on themes that preoccupied him. The two younger authors arrogantly romanticized World War II, while the elder navigated the murky waters of the Vichy regime. By the mid-1960s, Morand had not yet escaped purgatory and the *Hussards* in general seemed relegated to the past; Blondin wrote his last work, *Un singe en hiver,* in 1959, and Nimier died in a car accident in 1962. The New Novel was the future, as the literary magazine *Tel Quel* confirmed. However, several literary events revealed the lingering *Hussard* presence. For example, in the spring of 1965, the collection *Journées de lecture* brought Nimier back into a spotlight that he never really left. *L'étrangère,* a previously unpublished novel written in his youth, came out at the same time as *La place de l'étoile.* In 1970, Blondin published his book, *Monsieur Jadis,* in which Nimier figured heavily. Bernard Frank, who had founded the group fifteen years previously, also ended his silence with *Un siècle débordé.* In this lengthy and digressive chronicle, he invokes his own literary debuts while simultaneously criticizing Modiano. He stipulated that luck played heavily in Modiano's winning of two awards

14. Modiano, *Vestiaire de l'enfance* (Paris: Gallimard, Folio 2253, [1989] 2009), 97. My emphasis.
15. "Paul Morand, un revenant," 91. My emphasis.
16. *Ibid.*
17. Denis Cosnard, *Dans la peau de Patrick Modiano* (Paris: Fayard, 2010), 42.

(also mentioning the Prix Fénéon) for his first novel, which he claims is simply a remake or appropriation of the "mental mechanism" of two pre-existing works (Nimier's *Les épées* and Frank's own *Israël*).[18] Frank's reaction to the situation was lighthearted, even complicit, demanding only a case of champagne in terms of reparations. Modiano would be equally cordial that autumn when he responded with a three-page journal article entitled "L'anti-Frank," wherein he was so brazen in his brio and flattery that the end result was neither hostile nor "anti." Indeed, Modiano's paradoxical title is actually a subtle play on the fact that Frank was a contrarian. The fact that he is "anti" by nature suggests that one must be "pro-Frank" to be effectively "anti-Frank." Among the compliments, and veiled criticisms, Modiano praises the return of the *Hussards*, boasting that "after all, it's not every day that famous literary cartoons decide to leave their frames and talk to us without the use of speech bubbles."[19] Literary greats or cartoon clowns? Are they more famous or foolish? Are "bubbles" a reference to child's play or to the observation balloons of *Hussard* lore? This playful and misleading approach gives Modiano the upper hand. However, while sparing Frank he succeeds in making a mockery of Butor and Sollers, the New Novel and *Tel Quel*, implying that their work is little more than ridiculous invention; the only way they could ever win in a contest against Proust, Joyce, and Faulkner, he adds, would be at the Concours Lépine.[20] This rejection of contemporary avant-garde literature clearly pushes the limits of casual joking. Modiano even goes so far as to propose that a Bernard Frank club be founded in Tunis where—*quelle horreur !*—Frank's books are not sold. We see here that Modiano has clearly taken sides, showing a casual and distant preference, but a preference nonetheless.

In terms of works and readings, how can "The Occupation Trilogy" be linked to the *Hussards*? Modiano himself denies any influences on his work, and not without just cause. Yet one link that might be considered is that they all contest "official" history. Indeed, the *Hussards* refuse to accept history as told by the victors in 1945. According to them, only a small minority of writers had a true commitment to

18. Bernard Frank, *Un siècle débordé* (Paris: Bernard Grasset, 1969), 238.
19. Modiano, "L'anti-Frank," *Contrepoint* 2 (1970): 178.
20. The Concours Lépine is a very old (at least a century) contest for inventors of gadgets like vegetable shredders, vacuum cleaners, electric wheelchairs, and (more recently) electronic widgets. [—eds.]

the Resistance—and likewise to Collaboration. Far from what contemporary mythologies led people to believe, the Liberation and the false victory of 1945, paired with the pseudo-justice of racial purification, marked the victory of opportunism and recantation. This was a blatant lie, a generation of adults "playing the part," and a complete reversal of moral values. World War II, as proposed by Blondin in *L'Europe buissonnière* (1949) and by Nimier in *Les épées* (1948) and *Le Hussard bleu* (1950), is represented in a carnivalesque and nonchalant way. The *Hussard* (or hussar) is a libertine who rejects the activist and contrasts him with the adventurer.[21] Diametrically opposed to Sartrean heroes, characters in the works of *Hussard* novelists move across the pitfalls of history with a roguish cynicism, cultivating an attitude of disrespect and insolence toward the previous generations. This may be where the corrosive vision of the French Occupation presented in Modiano's trilogy finds its roots, although if not, it certainly represents a comparable precedent. In both cases, a generation stands up to its forefathers who fabricated history to suit their own interests. However, the contentious approach of the *Hussards*, which stems from an ideological foundation and heritage, is in stark contrast to Modiano's imaginary Third Republic and French colonial empire, tinged with the nationalistic tendencies of *Action française*. For Modiano, this ideological backdrop becomes a source of satire, fantasy, and delirium, whereas for the *Hussards* it motivates a response, not only a humorous and ironic response, but also a reactionary one.

    Their other point of similarity is on a more literary plane. If Modiano chose to tell a story through characters and a subjective lens, these conventions, condemned by Robbe-Grillet as outdated, are common in the works of *Hussard* writers. In 1962, Nimier wrote: "Whether they be English, American, or French, today's young literary minds have three gods: Proust, Céline, and Joyce."[22] Modiano would doubtless have replaced Joyce with Genet, but these "three gods" sufficed to inspire his move toward a freestyle narration centered on expression of the self. At the very height of the New Novel, both

---

    21. See François-Jean Authier, "Partis pris sans parti, ou la fantasmatique hussarde du militant chez Michel Déon et Jacques Laurent," and Dambre, "Du militant au libertin : les premiers romans de Blondin et de Nimier," in *Fiction et engagement politique. La représentation du parti et du militant dans le roman et le théâtre du XXe siècle*, ed. Jeanyves Guérin, (Paris: Presses Sorbonne Nouvelle, 2008), 179–89 and 147–57.
    22. Nimier, *L'élève d'Aristote*, ed. Dambre (Paris: Gallimard, 1981), 282.

Modiano and the *Hussards* defied popular conventions in contrast to the avant-garde movement, which Modiano did not take seriously. This choice only reinforced his personal writing style and tone. The importance that Modiano places on subjectivity creates an esthetic of insolent humor and irony wherein provocation features heavily. This is clearly the case in *La place de l'étoile*.

NOTABLE HUSSARDIAN PRECEDENTS

These two common denominators make Modiano a "free agent" of the *Hussard* generation. He is clearly in their wake, despite the fact that he is swimming against the current. For example, some specific traits point to an implicit dialogue with his forebears, a dialogue full of contrasts and oppositions.

As mentioned above, when Bernard Frank demanded a case of champagne in exchange for his services, he had in mind his 1955 book *Israël*. Indeed, true to the tone of this essay, its first words may be reflective of Raphaël Schlemilovitch's defiant position:

> Upon leaving Tel-Aviv, my distain flared. I kept telling anyone who would listen how bored I was with captain Dreyfus and his petty af-fairs, justice in particular. I was quick to add: "We cannot defend an officer, an Alsatian brown-noser." Although, one day I did persuade myself that Dreyfus had indeed committed treason and that Israeli gold alone had bought Zola, Clemenceau, and even the military tri-bunals. I took steps to have a handsome statue of him erected, like the one of Marechal Foch, in Tel-Aviv's main square. The children of Israel need no longer be jealous of France's cult of Marshal Pétain."[23]

This period in history is filled with questions surrounding Jewish identity, double-dealings, and the potential for backlash and betrayal. Here, the boundaries of history are pushed beyond the constraints imposed by modern society, and social conventions are ignored or defied. The fantasy of "I" gives the author free rein to express him-self with insolence, authority, and an unapologetic refusal to con-form. Showing disloyalty to Dreyfus, portraying his supporters and the military tribunals as corrupt, conflating Dreyfus with Pétain: all these provocations launched by Frank, himself a Jew, are reminiscent of the "mental mechanics" typical of a Modiano character. Did this precedent encourage Modiano? Regardless, the fine blend of classical

23. Frank, *Géographie universelle* suivi de *Israël* (Paris: Flammarion, 1989), 251.

and baroque styles that characterizes *La place de l'étoile* contrasts sharply with the uncontrolled loquaciousness that makes reading *Israël* so exhausting and tedious.

That Modiano took Roger Nimier as a model for Jean-François des Essarts, a prominent character in *La place de l'étoile*, is strongly suggested by a whole network of interconnections. The character bears Modiano's original first name, Jean, and his adoption of François instead of Patrick links the character to François Saint-Anne and François Sanders, the protagonists of *Les épées* and *Le Hussard bleu*. Both novels involve an exchange of identities: under false papers, Nimier's character becomes Lévy, "born in Geneva, July 30, 194 . . . ," while Schlemilovitch becomes "des Essarts." This identity swop makes further reference to Nimier's *Enfants tristes*, a novel "dedicated to the memory of Henri Mosseri (1924–1944)," a choice that surprised Modiano, who dedicated several of his own early novels to his brother, Rudy, also lost too soon. This confirms what Bruno Blanckeman suggests regarding survivor's guilt and the persistent memories of the early, traumatic death of a brother.[24] The dedications cross paths and refer directly to each other.

Regarding the narrative techniques in *La place de l'étoile*, a novel of the Liberation and also Modiano's literary debut, Blanckeman has clearly shown the ambiguous homage Modiano pays to the *Hussards*. Nimier in particular was honored with two pastiches, both associated with criticism of *Journées de lecture*, which had recently been published. Modiano transposes the scholastic concept of parallelism used by Nimier, and employs the term "parallèle" to describe Peugeot and Citroën cars.[25] Elsewhere, Des Essarts' advice mirrors the advice Nimier gives with regard to Louise de Vilmorin: reading is depicted as a combination of refined taste and *art de vivre*.[26] However, Modiano distances himself from the kind of "dandy" pretentiousness he finds frivolous and outdated. His work draws from forgotten authors such as René Boylesve, Édouard Estaunié, and Abel Hermant,[27] reading Jouhandeau, Chardonne, and Morand, for example. Yet, contrary to complaints of dandyism, Sartre's *What is literature?*, which targeted

24. Bruno Blanckeman, "Nimier dans le rétroviseur. Sur *La Place de l'étoile*," *Roger Nimier Cahier de l'Herne* 99 (2012): 120.
25. *La place de l'étoile*, 54.
26. *Journées de lecture* I, "Louise de Vilmorin" (Paris: Gallimard, 2015), 269–70.
27. *La place de l'étoile*, 38.

Des Essarts, constitutes both a subtle playfulness (perceived as a resolute opponent of Sartre, Nimier nonetheless dedicated *L'étrangère* to him, just as Des Essarts dedicated his essay to Sartre) and a flattering, yet evasive, response. Unquestionably, though, *Journées de lecture* seems to better respond to Sartre's question. In its first version, *La place de l'étoile* is directed as much against Sartre as against Céline.[28]

For reasons that will not be discussed here, the preface by Jean Cau was removed in the later publications of *La place de l'étoile*. Cau, while not widely read today, received the Prix Goncourt in 1961 and should not be overlooked. As a long-time enemy of the *Hussards*, he published a book in 1965 that revived and exacerbated the themes developed by *Hussard* authors fifteen years earlier. In Cau's *Le meurtre d'un enfant*, a story told in the first person and presented as non-autobiographical, the narrator vehemently opposes the glossed-over vision of World War II meant to create unanimity. Certain passages of Cau's work triggered strong controversies, for example:

> The infinitesimal minority of resistance fighters were never able to raise the groveling people off their knees, a people dumbed down by the reign of Édouard Daladier and the *opérettes marseillaises*. Cracked were the bells that tolled the Liberation. Is that how Rebatet or Céline would talk?[29]

La place de l'étoile starts in much the same way: the vengeful and moralizing Liberation and the illusions of 1940 and 1945 are also denounced: "The Liberation had come. We acted *as if* we had won the war. Young people of today, sons and daughters of the Allied victory (the Good) over the Nazis (the Bad), you did not experience, as we did, the false victory and the false defeat."[30] Betrayal became an obsession, and identifying with the Jews or the SS led to retrospective guilt. Modiano must have read *Le meurtre d'un enfant*, published by Gallimard. Reading this book today, we immediately conclude that the choice of Cau to write the preface was not without some literary basis.

---

28. In addition to other arguments, this is what Stéphane Chaudier suggests: "'J'étais un vrai jeune homme.' L'édition revue et corrigée de *La place de l'étoile*," *Europe* 1038 (October 2015): 39.

29. Jean Cau, *Le meurtre d'un enfant* (Paris: Gallimard, 1965), 28.

30. *Ibid.*, 45–46.

CONCLUSION

Paul Morand made a name for himself during the period following World War I, whereas authors such as Roger Nimier, Jean Cau,
and Bernard Frank came to the literary forefront after World War II.
Through their work, these four writers contributed to Modiano's travels through history, facilitating his communication with generations
past. This would lead Modiano to further success with *Lacombe Lucien*, co-written with Louis Malle, a friend and admirer of Roger Nimier with whom he made his first film, *Ascenseur pour l'échafaud*.
This approach to history allowed Modiano to delve more deeply into
the troubled times that haunted his memory and motivated his quest.

Modiano owes little to Morand, not even the conversations that
he dreamed of having about his friend Marcel Proust, who wrote the
preface to Morand's *Tendres stocks* in 1921. But he encountered the
Hussard spirit early on, becoming acquainted with it through reading
the weekly cultural newspaper *Arts*,[31] which was headed by Jacques
Laurant for many years before being run by Nimier from 1959 to
1961. Modiano was familiar with the kind of liberty associated with
the great classics, disrespect for trends, and the sense of initiative that
made the publication a staunch supporter of New Wave cinema.[32]
Through the influential novels that characterize the movement, he
was introduced to a "libertine" vision of the war that rejected postwar myths and the dominant parties behind their creation. It also
seems clear that Nimier's *Les épées* was a major influence, as was the
powerful appeal of his criticism and persona. But, with time and age,
the *Hussards* fell below Modiano's horizon. Their mentality was of
another era, and their literary giants hardly a reference for greatness
when held up against Proust, Genet, or Céline.

—Translated from the French by Marie Claire Chao

31. See, for example, *Un pedigree* (Paris, Gallimard, Folio 4377, 2014), 71.
32. See *Arts 1952–1966 : la culture de la provocation*, ed. Henri Blondet (Paris,
Tallandier, 2009).

VAN KELLY

Mapping Self and/as Other: Attempts to Fuse Horizons in Modiano and Le Clézio

> When you enter a book, you leave a part of yourself and you gain a part of someone else.
>
> —J-M G. Le Clézio[1]

The two recent French winners of the Nobel Prize for Literature— Patrick Modiano since *Les boulevards de ceinture* (1972), and J-M G. Le Clézio beginning especially with *Désert* (1982)—relentlessly explore whether it is legitimate, and if so, to what degree, for an intradiegetic narrator to fuse with, or voice empathetically as if from within, the consciousness and life circumstances of other characters, to merge imaginarily with or to adopt parts of those other characters' identites, in an effort to relive their dilemmas within history. The ontological enigmas that such attempted mind-mergers and era-transfers harbor—the dramas of living for a time within the internal focus of another character, to the point of confusing one's sense of self with that character—bring Modiano's and Le Clézio's worlds momentarily into partial union, only to disjoin them fundamentally, as I will argue in relation to Modiano's *Voyage de noces (Honeymoon)* (1990) and Le Clézio's *Étoile errante (Wandering Star)* (1992). These novels probe, in ways that project their distinct worldviews, the limits of crossover into another's mind, and blockages to transfer into another's skin, even in fiction. *Voyage de noces* and *Étoile errante* both occur under the shadow of the Shoah.

---

1. "Postscript: ""Doubting must be the beginning of wisdom.' A Conversation with J. M. G. Le Clézio, Albuquerque, New Mexico, July 2011," in Keith Moser, *J. M. G. Le Clézio: A Concerned Citizen of the Global Village* (Plymouth, UK: Lexington Books, 2013), 193.

YFS 133, *"Detecting" Patrick Modiano*, ed. Golsan and Higgins, © 2018 by Yale University.

In *Voyage de noces*, Modiano underscores the Shoah's aftereffects on Ingrid Teyrsen, debilitated by a tragic choice linked to her father's deportation and death, and on Jean B., who did not experience World War II and whose career as an adventure filmmaker is, at best, melodramatic. The plot's twists suggest that the gap between catastrophe and postwar imagination of it is insuperable. Le Clézio creates a tri-focal perspective for his characters, conjoining Esther Grève's escape from racial persecution in World War II France with her migration to Palestine at the moment of Israel's independence, and then with Palestinian refugee crisis in the aftermath of the 1948 Arab-Israeli war. This crisis affects Nejma, a Palestinian whom Esther meets briefly, introducing a different sort of ethical, ideological bind, since Nejma is on her way to exile in refugee camps in Jordan. Modiano's literary horizon rarely exceeds the span between 1940 and the publication dates of his novels, whereas Le Clézio's novels, multiplying colonial and postcolonial legends, often embrace centuries (from the French Revolution to the 1968 Olympic Games, for instance, in his 1997 novel *Révolutions*). Furthermore, staging the Occupation, while unremarkable for Modiano, is exceptional for Le Clézio who spent his childhood in wartime France, but centers most of his novels elsewhere, in his family's Mauritian and North African pasts, and in his own experiences in Nigeria and Latin America. In *Étoile errante*, though, Le Clézio operates in Modiano's *chasse gardée*. The time span, 1943 until 1982, largely overlays that of Modiano's *Voyage de noces*, 1941 to 1989. Both novels hinge on the possibilities of deep, hospitable connections with the Other in the aftermath of World War II, but the characters resist merging. How each author attempts to link the minds of co-sympathetic characters, but more importantly, how each reacts when the experiment in mind-merger encounters impedance and even failure is crucial to understanding their evolution as writers who place ethics, history, and hospitality at the heart of their post-*Nouveau roman* return to problems of ontological characterization and psychological identity.

To depict characters fractured by history's crises, Modiano and Le Clézio complicate story strands and interrelationships by arranging for the primary focalizing consciousness, Jean B. or Esther, each with a multilayered past, to encounter a rival consciousness, Ingrid Teysen or Nejma, each harboring an equally if not more reverberative counter-past. To build this crosshatching, Modiano and Le Clézio create chance encounters (Jean B. encounters Ingrid around 1965 on the Côte d'Azur, 1968 in Paris, and 1971 in Milan, and Esther meets Nejma near Jerusalem in 1948) which, even after the other character disappears (Ingrid's suicide, Nejma's fade toward Jordan), haunt the primaries, Jean B. and Esther, who try to make the paths that led to the original meeting coincide again by other means. Ingrid and Nejma become a co-destiny for Jean B. and Esther respectively—they yearn to revivy the pact of mutual protection that the path-crossing implied. Something in the circumstances, though, relating to the dangers Ingrid and Nejma face, prevents these attempts to recreate solidarity from becoming truly effective.[2]

JEAN B. AND INGRID TEYRSEN

Modiano's overlapping, or superimposition, of two different lives one upon the other often turns on attempts by internal narrators like Jean B. in *Voyage de noces* to merge their consciousness with that of key players in a compromised, dangerous past. These homodiegetic narrators (they play a role in the story they recount) frequently become, *in medias res*, autodiegetic (the story shifts toward their self-definition, through focalization on the story's farthest past stratum). The ambitious scope of Modiano's experimentation in superimposition and merging of disparate minds and eras is visible in earlier novels, especially in *Les boulevards de ceinture, Rue des boutiques obscures*, and *Quartier perdu*; but the ending of *Voyage de noces*, where the plot cascades from Ingrid's disastrous past to Jean B.'s deficient present, unmasks in a new way the historical scope and ethical stakes of absorptive characterization that attempts to fuse the identities of interrelated characters. Modiano concludes *Voyage de noces* with one of his signature tempos—the effortless dreamlike bicycle ride, as Jean B. revisits the places in northeastern Paris where the plot has unfolded, connecting his life from 1965 to 1989 with those of World War II survivors Paul Rigaud and Ingrid Teyrsen from 1941 to 1971. These two strands intersect, creating territorial overlays, that is, partial union sets symptomatic of what Bruno Blanckeman

---

2. Cf. Walter Putnam, "The Poetics and Politics of Space in J. M. G. Le Clézio's *Étoile errante*," in *Borders, Exiles, Diasporas*, ed. E. Barkan and M.-D. Shelton (Stanford: Stanford UP, 1998), 315; and Bruno Thibault, *J. M. G. Le Clézio et la métaphore exotique* (Amsterdam: Rodopi, 2009), 167, 172. Both find balance between Esther and Nejma.

calls the "porousness of being" typical of Modiano's characters.[3] The page before this bicycle ride, Jean B. has finished his re-imagination of Ingrid's choice in the Paris winter of 1941–1942: during a Franco-German dragnet in the 18th arrondissement, she decided not to cross the police line and abandoned her father in their *hôtel meublé*. After attempts to find her, including placing a missing person's notice in a newspaper, her father disappeared amid French racial deportations. Ingrid, despite a tardy attempt to recontact him, joined Rigaud, her protector, fleeing from la Place de l'étoile, to Paris's periphery, to the Riviera in the "unoccupied" zone, and beyond, to survival.

But fully understanding Jean B.'s reconstitution of Ingrid's past depends on the link to another Modiano signature scene: the moment, a third of the way through the novel, when the intradiegetic narrator throws away his meticulous but incomplete documentation: "I didn't need to consult my notes that evening . . . I remembered everything as if it had been yesterday" (38). As Alan Morris asks, is this "reconstruction through knowledge? Or reconstruction through fantasy ?"[4] What Jean B. is "remembering" is an Occupation he had not experienced, which he relives fusionally through a hypotyposis or vivid simulation of the past, as if he were denying the vicariousness of his relationship to Ingrid's war experiences, merging his consciousness with hers. Ingrid's story ended with her suicide in Milan in 1971. This incites Jean B. to re-imagine her passage through the war in three segments given in reverse chronological order: her escape with Rigaud to the Zone Libre in the spring 1942, and their survival until the war's end; the sixteen year-old Ingrid's fatal choice on "one of the last days in November [1941]" (93), her meeting that same day with Rigaud, and their flight to the 12th arrondissement; and, finally, a revisiting of events from November 1941 through early 1942 ("The snow had melted and it was so mild you could go out without a coat" [117]), namely Ingrid's father's newspaper ad published just before his deportation "about the middle of December [1941]" (117), and her belated visit in early 1942 to the hotel, Boulevard Ornano, where she discovers the tragedy, before fleeing Paris.

Intercalated between the three phases of this staggered sequence of flashbacks are Jean B.'s own experiences in modern prepipheral Paris

3. Bruno Blanckeman, *Lire Patrick Modiano* (Paris: Armand Colin, 2009), 162, my trans.
4. Alan Morris, *Patrick Modiano* (Oxford, UK: Berg, 1996), 171.

in the Hôtel Dodds near Porte Dorée and then in what he assumes to be Rigaud's old apartment on Boulevard Soult, which he rents clandestinely. Documents from Jean B.'s *chemise cartonnée*, a folder that represents many years of patient research, serve as trailmarkers for this backward march into the estranging past of Ingrid and Rigaud. A false civil marriage certificate, which is part of the new couple's alias, anchors the first flashback, the scenes of refuge in the south in 1942–1944. The discovery of a new document in the apartment on Boulevard Soult—the public announcement on January 12, 1942 of the imminent sale of the building near the Place de l'étoile on rue de Tilsitt where Rigaud's mother had been a tenant—spurs the second flashback, which recounts Ingrid's choice and her encounter with Rigaud in a *salon de thé*. The third flashback, to Ingrid's final visit to the hotel on Boulevard Ornano where the owner informs her of her father's deportation is tied to a third document, which Jean B. does not obtain until 1968, the missing person's ad which implicitly compelled Ingrid to recontact her father, but too late. None of the flashbacks belongs to Jean B.'s own, direct memory, though each contains moments of internal focalization, either on Rigaud (large segments of the first flashback to their refuge in Juan-les-Pins and nearby) or on Ingrid (several spots in the second and third ones, which recount her choice and its immediate consequences). These are the only times we are afforded a point of view, or *caméra subjective*, from the perspectives of protector Rigaud and psychologically-wounded Ingrid. Yet it is the internal focalization in these characters that dialogizes Jean B.'s mind, creating what Bakhtine calls "words that stubbornly resist" an author's capture, "sounding foreign in the mouth of the one who appropriated them and who now speaks them; they cannot be assimilated into his context . . . as if they put themselves in quotations marks against the will of the author."[5] Jean B., the self-appointed teller of the couple's tale, struggles to assimilate these voices and build a threshold of merger with their thoughts and feelings, although hearing Ingrid's inner motivation is Jean B.'s primordial quest.

Jean B.'s absorption of, and into, the minds of his characters is punctuated by withdrawals from Ingrid and Rigaud's wartime plane of diegesis, when he consults his *chemise cartonnée* or meets characters from his modern Parisian life, such as Ben Smidane, who comes

5. M.M. Bakhtin, *The Dialogic Imagination: Four Essays*, trans. C. Emerson and M. Holquist (Austin: University of Texas Press, 1981), 294.

as emissary from Annette, Jean B.'s wife. But there is a more important foil for Jean's fusional, internally dialogized relivings of Ingrid's
Occupation: three separate and distinct flashbacks, to 1965, 1968, and
1971, which, by contrast, belong to Jean B.'s own zone of lived experience and memory. They, too, are presented in reverse chronological
order—1971, 1965, 1968—and they constitute the true-life intersection between Jean B. (before he became the present-day narrator of
Ingrid's story) and the couple, Ingrid and Rigaud.

The first flashback, to 1971, opens the novel *in medias res*, when
during a stop in Milan's train station, Jean B. learns about the suicide
of a woman on her way to Capri. Later, when he reads the obituaries
in *Il corriere della sera*, he learns that the woman was Ingrid Teyrsen,
whom he knew. His reaction to the suicide provides the impulse for
his quest, which structures the novel: "Perhaps there was a motive
for this gesture that I would never know" (*Voyage de noces*, 13, my
translation). This episode opens up an eighteen-year gap, or fuzzy
zone, in the explicit record of events in Jean B.'s own life, between
1971 and 1989, during which, we can infer, he has been gathering the
documents that he hopes will lead to uncovering the "reason" for her
suicide. This gap, though it is clearly not the result of a subconscious
forgetting or repression, nevertheless signals Jean B.'s critical invest-
ment in this (in)quest. In the novel's last pages, Ingrid's truth will return to strike Jean B. with all the force of the return of the repressed,
due to the powers of psychic fusion that he, sleuth-turned-narrator,
has applied to imagining her wartime dilemma. The memory of this
trip to Milan in 1971 and what he learned there lead Jean B. to iso-
late himself in Paris; he retreats from his wife and friends in an attempt finally to solve Ingrid's mystery. Jean's first flashback to his
own lived experience leads to a second one, his idyllic encounter in
Saint-Raphaël, when he was twenty, circa 1965, with the older and
wizened Ingrid and Rigaud, who offer him shelter and companionship
for a day and a night, after which he returns to Paris.

But it is the final flashback of this series relating to Jean B.'s own
lived experience that draws the true axis of his encounters with Ingrid
and sets up, in the last sentence of the novel, the final scene depict-
ing the very strong empathy he feels for Ingrid, which leads him to
adopt a narrative voice that absorbs her imagined feelings, and merges
them with his own mindset. This flashback, where Jean B. recalls his
last encounter with Ingrid in 1968 in Paris, is divided into two parts.
The first recounts their coincidental meeting on avenue de Lowendal

near the École Militaire, and their subsequent dinner conversation about past and present. Only in the densely-packed last five pages of the novel is this flashback completed, filled in with the crucial piece of evidence, the missing person's ad placed by Ingrid's father, which she had kept for all those years: "I remember that at that moment she fell silent, and looked at me with a strange expression, as if she wanted to transfer to me a burden that had long weighed on her, or as if she guessed that I too, later, would go looking for her" (116). Immediately after Jean B. has completed this flashback, which gives him the missing key to understanding Ingrid's choice and trauma, he does indeed accept the transfer, and he imagines and relives Ingrid's tardy grief-inducing return to her father's hotel at 39bis Boulvard Ornano, with internal focalization on her thoughts; that is, Jean B. shifts the story to its other axis, the series of flashbacks to experiences he could not have lived and that belong authentically only to Ingrid. As he imagines her late visit to the hotel, this in turn sets up the critical fusional moment of the novel's last sentence in which Jean B. suggests that he, like Ingrid in 1971, is about to be pulled into a riptide, and may commit suicide. The flashback to 1968 sutures Jean B.'s banal, insouciant life to Ingrid's grieving life, striated with aftereffects of her decisions of 1941–1942. Without this flashback to his last lived encounter with Ingrid, Jean B.'s relationship with her would not have been transformative, and the second axis leading back to 1941–1942, the ethical core of *Voyage de noces*, would not have materialized. But in 1968, Jean B. inherited, and transferred into his own mindset, the strange accents and shards of Ingrid's trauma, as the novel's last page shows, contrasting ironically with Jean B.'s deceptively free-wheeling bicycle ride to Boulevard Ornano.

Jean B.'s book-long stint as sleuth and imaginer of Ingrid's wartime past is, in the final moment of his bicycle ride, firmly linked to his own state of mind. When he stops in front of the hotel where Ingrid and her father once lived, he empathizes with the "sense of emptiness" (119) he imagines Ingrid felt when the hotel owner indicated that her father had been deported to "he didn't know where" (117).[6] The catastrophic feeling in the novel's closing paragraph is not Ingrid's alone, since intradiegetic narrator Jean B. fuses the supposition of *her* inner emptiness with his own crisis: he becomes an autodiegetic

6. Patrick Modiano, *Honeymoon*, trans. Barbara Wright (Boston: David R. Gadine, 1995), 120, 117; Patrick Modiano, *Voyage de noces* (Paris: Gallimard, 1990), 157.

narrator, one discovering his own self-definition. "X" marks the spot: this catastrophic feeling is the intersection point of the two series of flashbacks, ones based on events Jean B. had lived, and others he had imagined from Ingrid's intimate life, based on documents and, more importantly, crafted with his writer's gift for mind merging with the other's internal focus. To use Seymour Chatman's terms, Jean B.'s idiosyncratic "slant" as narrator, and the mindset or inner "filter" he has imagined for Ingrid's attitudes and perceptions in 1941 and afterwards, are superimposed one upon the other and, in the novel's last three words, form a full union of their two minds and a merger of their respective dilemmas and despair: "Circumstances and settings are of no importance. One day this sense of emptiness and remorse submerges you. Then, like a tide, it ebbs and disappears. But in the end it returns in force, and she couldn't shake it off. *Nor could I*" (120, emphasis added).[7] Readers who fully accept Jean B.'s absorption of Ingrid's desperate mindset, and interpret his final words as a mind- and life-merger with Ingrid, might conclude that he will imitate Ingrid down to her last act. (But this ending is also earmarked by Modiano's playfulness, the suggestion, for instance, made just before the final "Nor could I," that Jean B. may instead return to his wife, Annette, in Cité Véron.) Jean B. formulates a plausible, true-life explanation for Ingrid's despair, yet imbalance remains between the ethical weight of her choice and his fantastical sleuthing to re-establish her story, not to mention his final melodramatic image of drowning under the riptide of sympathy that overtakes him during his quest. This imbalance opens the door for the real-life alternative to *Voyage de noces*, *Dora Bruder*, where the psychic intermediary Jean B. will disappear from the diegesis.

ESTHER AND NEJMA

In *Étoile errante*, Le Clézio also tries to depict an overlaying or superimposition of identities in the aftermath of World War II and the Shoah, although in a very different ideological context from Modiano's. In 1988, Le Clézio published part of the novel, "Camp de Nour Shams, été 1948," in the *Revue d'études palestiniennes*, which roused controversy: Guy Scarpetta and Bernard-Henri Lévy accused

---

7. Seymour Chatman, *Coming to Terms: The Rhetoric of Narrative in Fiction and Film* (Ithaca, NY: Cornell University Press, 1990), 142–54

Le Clézio of writing a pro-Palestinian, anti-Israeli screed, which he denied.[8] The parts of *Étoile errante* devoted to Nejma originated in Le Clézio's horror on reading U.N. reports on conditions in Palestinian refugee camps. The book shows "adolescents undergoing a crisis [*une épreuve*] not uniquely linked" to the 1948 war but portraying the "lack of understanding one often feels in the middle of catastrophe."[9] Le Clézio tied the novel to his childhood in occupied France: "To have been born in 1940 is to have grown up with the ingrained feeling that violence is always imminent."[10]

Esther's legal name is Hélène Grève, but her true, Jewish name was given to her by her father, a martyr of the Jewish Resistance in Haute-Savoie, killed by the Gestapo as he conveyed Jewish refugees over the Italian border. Esther's postwar immigration to Palestine with her mother Élisabeth takes the reader into the maelstrom of the 1948 Arab-Israeli war. Esther's co-protagonist is Nejma. With the help of an extradiegetic implied author who splices sequences and shifts between narrative points of view,[11] the women's plots converge on their encounter somewhere near Latrun, between Jaffa (Tel Aviv's twin Arab city) and greater Jerusalem.[12] Nejma is fleeing her native city of Acre (Akka, between Haïfa and the Lebanese border) and heading toward Jordan's West Bank and, eventually, to the refugee camp Nur Shams (near Tulkarm). Esther's convoy is going to Jerusalem, and later to the kibbutz Ramat Yohanon (close to Haifa). This itinerary,

8. J. M. G. Le Clézio, "Camp de Nour Shams, été 1948," *Revue des études palestiniennes* 29 (1988): 3–34. Marina Salles synopsizes the polemic in *Le Clézio, notre contemporain* (Rennes: Presses Universitaires de Rennes, 2006), 50–51. See also Thibault, 165–67.

9. Françoise Ducout, "Les cicatrices intérieures de Le Clézio," Interview, *Elle* (May 11, 1992): 44, my translation.

10. Jérôme Garcin, *Littérature vagabonde* (Paris: Flammarion, 1995), 278, my translation.

11. On the implied author, see Wayne C. Booth, *The Rhetoric of Fiction* (1961; rpt. Chicago: University of Chicago Press, 1973), 149–165; and Chatman, 74–108.

12. Le Clézio, *Wandering Star*, trans. C. Dickson (Willimantic, CT: Curbstone, 2004), 308. Unless otherwise indicated, English quotations from *Étoile errante* (Paris: Gallimard, 1992) are from this translation. On the rich ambiguity in Nejma's and Esther's geographic descriptions of the place of their encounter, see Matthew Moyle, "Récits cartographes, cartes palimpsests" in *Cartographier les récits*, ed. M. Fournier (Clermont-Ferrand: Presses universitaires Blaise Pascal, 2016), 78–79. As Moyle notes, Esther talks of "the road toward Siloam" (*Wandering Star*, 308), Nejma of the "road to the Latrun Spring" (208). Both Latrun and Siloam were crossed by the U.N. green line separating warring parties at armistice, underscoring the "precariousness of their encounter" (Moyle, 79).

as Mathew Moyle suggests, maps the "inequality between the two young women" and emphasizes Esther's "freedom of movement" (80). At their meeting, Nejma approaches Esther and creates a cooperative game amid ongoing war:

> . . . she wrote her name, in capital letters like this: N E J M A. She handed the notebook and the pencil to Esther, so that she too would write down her name. She stood there for a moment longer, hugging the notebook to her breast, as if it were the most important thing in the world. Finally, without saying a word, she went back toward the group of refugees. . . . Esther took a step toward her, to call her, to hold her back, but it was too late. (193)

This moment of encounter, beyond the novel's midpoint, orients *Étoile errante* toward the identity overlay, or transmigration of souls, hidden in its title: Nejma in Arabic means "star," and Esther's nickname, given by her father, is Estrellita, "little star."[13] This single meeting and farewell initiate identity confusion, which is the novel's main focus, a "painful alternation of attachments and violent separations" (Thibault, 182), a "severing as well as merging of both strands."[14] After the exchange, Esther and Nejma go their separate ways, but attempt to communicate with the lost sister-soul through writing: "[P]sychic space supersedes physical space" (Putnam, 323). Nejma spends harsh months at Nur Shams, then flees with Saadi and baby Loula to Jordan and other camps. The implied author deprives us of knowledge of Nejma's future, except for her diary's opening, which suggests she alone survived the exodus. Esther has no more information about Nejma, yet starts a diary with her as the implicit adressee. The meeting "reconfigures the intrinsic possibilities" of Esther's world and opens her mind to dialogism.[15]

Further appearances of Nejma's notebook, and of the other notebooks that Esther imagines or actually acquires in imitation of Nejma, "stage a process of opening and fissuring, of non-coincidence with

13. On the title, and geopolitical versus "nonquadrant" space, see Putnam, 312, 318–22.

14. Jean-Philippe Imbert, "J.-M. G. Le Clézio, Writer of Exile: A Treatment of Childhood in *Désert* and *Étoile errante*" in *Exiles and Migrants: Crossing Thresholds in European Culture and Society*, ed. Anthony Coulson (Brighton, UK: Sussex Academy Press, 1997), 204.

15. Justine Feyereisen, "Le regard des enfants d'*Étoile errante*," in *J. M. G. Le Clézio, explorateur des royaumes de l'enfance*, ed. N. Pien and D. Lanni (Paris: Passages, 2014), 135, my translation.

oneself" (Thibault, 182), which progressively enables the characters' attempts to merge psyches. "Hélène," the title of the novel's first part, traces her family's wartime hiding in Saint-Martin-Vésubie, before she and her mother flee to Italy in 1943 when her father dies, and then, in stages, to the newly-declared state of Israel, where Esther and Nejma meet. In the next section, "Nejma," dated 1948 at U.N. camp Nur Shams, Nejma writes her story, in the original notebook and several others, hoping that Esther will read them and seek her out.

When Nejma and her lover Saadi flee Nur Shams, her diary ends, replaced by an extradiegetic third-person narration. Nejma and Saadi find a haven amid battles on the West Bank, spending time in the valley of Azzoun, in the shade of acacias and olive trees, where "[b]ats appeared in the gray sky and took their turn at skimming over the deep pool of water" (258), a phrase that returns at novel's end, in Esther's mind. We last see Nejma and Saadi as they trek toward Amman, but Nejma's presence continues to permeate the novel. In the third part, "Child of the Sun," while at the kibbutz in 1950, Esther copies Yiddish poems into "the same kind [of notebook] in which Nejma had written her name" (273), moving herself into mental overlay with Nejma. The talismanic, mediumistic status of the notebook is reinforced when Esther writes a letter expressing her anguish: "maybe she was writing it for Nejma, on the same black notebook she had gotten out amid the dust of the road" (298). Esther's notebook is a simulacrum of Nejma's original one, it is a product of Esther's internal identity maneuvers and her thought bifurcated between love for Israel and love for Nejma, and it insinuates a multipolar consciousness of interpenetrating existences.[16]

A last avatar of Nejma's notebook appears in Montréal, in 1966, as Esther prepares her return to Israel with her son Michel, fruit of her union with Israeli soldier Jacques Berger who died in postwar violence. Esther dreams of Nejma's presence, and that Nejma's notebook reached her by mail or "mysterious messenger"(284). She can "decipher" what Nejma wrote "just for me, a story of love and wandering that could have been my own" (284). Esther buys "a black

16. On the "double cahier" and writing as reunion, see Jacqueline Michel, "Épreuves du livre. Réflexions sur *Étoile errante* de J. M. G. Le Clézio," *Lettres Romanes* 47/4 (1993): 284–85; and Silvia G. Sosa de Touyâa, "Voyages polyphoniques dans l'espace et dans le temps: *Désert* et *Étoile errante* de J. M. G. Le Clézio" in *Estudios argentinos de literatura francesa y francófona: Los viajes, los viajeros y el olvido*, ed. Universidad Nacional de Catamarca et al (Córdoba, Argentina: Comunicarte, 2004): 121.

notebook"(284), writes Nejma's name, and suggests a merger of their personal identies, via an allusion to Montaigne's language about his close friend La Boétie, in the essay "De l'amitié": "It was she, it was me, I no longer knew which.[17] One day, I would return to the road toward Siloam, and the cloud of dust would open, and Nejma would walk toward me. We would exchange our notebooks to abolish time, to extinguish the sufferings" (*Étoile errante*, 308, my translation). The original meeting's aftereffect is a binocular, merged vision of the women, but marked by elation, in contrast to Jean B.'s "Nor could I."[18] The interaction of all these notebooks maintains a zone where two sister souls unite.

The tensest stretch of *Étoile errante*'s plot is when Esther, as homodiegetic narrator, returns to Nice in 1982 to assist her dying mother. As Moyle notes, the places in this novel are like a "map-palimpsest" (81); they harbor and reveal, "prior layers" (80) of the characters' life experiences, "drawing the reader's attention to the exact place of the action and to another place" (81), "troubl[ing]" the characters' sense of place (81) and "lett[ing] the different strata dissimulated beneath the surface" appear (69). Esther's mind, as she walks along the port of Nice, brings two disparate images together, but they resist fusion; they resemble disjoint sets: "In the Var, seventeen thousand acres were in flame, there was a taste of ash in the air." "I saw women, children, slipping like shadows down the crumbling streets, the ruts of the refugee camps in Sabra, Chatila" (299). Brush fires burn the hilly Var; Lebanon burns during the 1982 Israeli invasion. Israeli occupation forces are close by; allied Lebanese Christian Phalangist militias massacre the Palestinian population of Sabra and Shatila.[19] Days later, the cremation of her mother's body makes Esther think of the deportation of Jews by the Gestapo and Vichy prefect of Nice, "to Drancy, and farther still, to Dachau, to Auschwitz" (301),

17. See Michel de Montaine, "Of Friendship," trans. Charles Cotton: "If a man should importune me to give a reason why I loved him, I find it could no otherwise be expressed, than by making answer: because it was he, because it was I."

18. On binocular vision, see Roger Shattuck, *Proust's Binoculars: A Study of Memory, Time, and Recognition in À la recherche du temps perdu* (New York: Random House, 1963).

19. On the Israeli invasion, Sabra and Shatila, and Lebanese and Israeli responsibility, see Bayan Nuwayhed Al-Hout, *Sabra and Shatila, September 1982* (London: Pluto Press, 2004), 297–324; and Elizabeth Picard, *Lebanon, A Shattered Clountry: Myths and Realities of the Wars in Lebanon*, trans. F. Philip (NY: Holmes and Meier, 2002), 123–26.

and as Esther visits sites of persecution in once occupied Nice (Hôtel Excelsior, Hôtel Hermitage), her mind brings the Israeli invasion of Lebanon into stark proximity with Franco-German atrocities under the Occupation. Beirut appears "transfixed in its destruction, the women and children of the refugee camps watch boats drifting away," while in Nice, "people . . . indifferent, remote . . . walk by corners where the martyred children were hung by the neck" (301). Esther's mind strains to correlate the two disparate, different sets of images of child victims. Her empathy for children spurs the two thoughts, but the fragility of the overlay between her "long journey toward her identity" as Isa van Acker says, and Nejma's journey toward "loss,"[20] is tangible within this torn internal focus.

This particular use of dialogization—the inner sounding of voices juxtaposing Esther's path with Nejma's—leads Le Clézio to construe a utopian ending fundamentally different from Jean B.'s final despair in *Voyage de noces*. The hope of reuniting with Nejma and retrieving her from the debris of past conflicts persists as Esther prepares to return to Israel, "my country where the light . . . shines most of all in the eyes of the children, the eyes from which I hope to drive all suffering . . . And I still think of Nejma, the sister I lost long ago . . . whom I must find again" (311). As the novel ends, and Esther disperses her mother's ashes at the seaside in Nice, she reconnects with the teenager she was, hopping gorges above Saint-Martin-Vésubie, before escaping to Italy: she "jumps from block to block along the jetty" (316). Young Nejma, too, rises again, a strangeness fusing with Esther's inner focus: "[Esther] feels immensely weary, immensely serene. *There are bats dancing around the lampposts*" (316, emphasis added). Nejma's internal view of the Azzoun where she found haven dialogizes Esther's mind. Esther can only possess this phrase through metempsychosis. Nejma, too, had anticipated this final merger with Esther. After her escape from Nur Shams, the waters of Azzoun remind her of her home in seaside Akka: "it had been so long since she'd felt such peace. She could dream . . . of the sea rolling over the rocks, of the cries of seagulls when the fishing boats neared the jetty" (257), replicating Esther's situation dockside in Nice in 1982.

---

20. Isa van Acker, "Polyphonie et altérité dans *Onitsha* et *Étoile errante*," in *Convergences and Interferences: Newness in Intercultural Practices*, ed. K. Gyssels, M. A. Bowers, and I. Hoving (Amsterdam: Rodopi, 2001): 206, my translation.

This virtuoso conlusion, which is highly empathetic and verges on a fusion of Esther's identity with Nejma's, vindicates Esther's desire for reconciliation, but points to a major imbalance. After years of violent severance, where is the other star, Nejma, materially? Esther finds new life in the places from which Nejma has been expelled and to which she is deprived of the right of return. The only union set between Esther and Nejma is that both were adolescents who suffered greatly through no fault of their own, from the prejudices and aspirations of others.[21] Esther never directly faces this imbalance except in her scene on the jetty in Nice, and during her crossroads contact with Nejma. As Nejma's convoy disappears, women around Esther invalidate her queries about the refugees' destination: "To Iraq"; "No one is innocent, they're the mothers and wives of the men who are killing us" (193–94). Her last words, "But what about the children?" (194), echo the novel's epigraph, "To the captured children," but no one answers.

DRAWING CONCLUSIONS FROM
NARRATIVE IMBALANCE

What Eric Auerbach calls "vertical connection" between plot lines, what "holds them together," cannot coax Jean B. and Ingrid, Esther and Nejma, into a convincing mind merger or psychic union where they would be as one, indistinguishable.[22]

In *Voyage de noces*, Modiano's longstanding favorite frame—a narration where present and cascading pasts are superimposed upon and pervade each other and are merged to varying degrees by an autodiegetic story-teller—leads him to a blunter confrontation with the Shoah, the catastrophe around which his prior works had maneuvered, only occasionally entering the grey zone (in *Lacombe Lucien*, for instance, with Albert Horn's surrender and deportation). When Modiano depicts Ingrid's true-life crisis, which could have led to the death camps but did not, and Dora Bruder's real-life deportation and death at Auschwitz alongside her father, Modiano's method of

21. In 1992, Le Clézio felt that the Arab-Israeli conflict could be resolved (Ducout, 44). See Moyle on the "ray of hope" which Esther's and Nejma's hopes for a future encounter, and and for a "beginning of peace," instill in the novel (81)

22. Erich Auerbach, *Mimesis: The Representation of Reality in Western Literature*, trans. Willard R. Trask, 4th ed. (1953; rpt. Princeton, NJ: Princeton University Press, 1974) 17.

retrospective merger and mind meld with the Occupation era reveals its weakness.

When Modiano wrote *Voyage de noces*, he had two factual documents concerning Dora: the missing-person notice placed by Ernst Bruder in the 31 December 1941 issue of *Paris Soir*, discovered by Modiano in 1988, and the record of her deportation, in her father's convoy on 18 September 1942, which he found in Serge Klarsfeld's *Le mémorial de la déportation des Juifs de France*.[23] The extreme "precision of certain details" in the missing-person notice, surrounded by "ignorance, forgetfulness, oblivion" of other information, haunted him. As he wrote *Voyage de noces*, he doubted he could ever convey her life story fully (*Dora Bruder*, 43). But after publication, other facts were discovered—with Klarsfeld's help, which created its own controversy[24]—and Modiano concluded that his exercise in empathy by fiction had touched real-life Dora at one insignificant point only: the first stop on Ingrid's and Rigaud's flight south, their apartment in the 12th arrondissement, close to the boarding school Dora had twice fled, putting herself in mortal danger (44).[25] *Dora Bruder*'s conclusion, underscoring what Modiano (for once) refused to imagine, reads like a denunciation of his own frequent, key device of fictional fusion or merger with prior eras and minds:

> I shall never know how she spent her days, where she hid, in whose company she passed the winter months of her first escape, or the few weeks of spring when she escaped for the second time. That is her secret. A poor and precious secret that not even the executioners, the decrees, the occupying authorities, the Dépôt, the barracks, the camps, History, time—everything that defiles and destroys you—have been able to take away from her. (119)

This shift unmasks Modiano's urge to fill the record's gaps, to get archival hegemony by all means. Jean B. re-imagined his "real-life" 1965 meeting with Ingrid and Rigaud; he also tried to fuse with the

23. Modiano, *Dora Bruder*, trans. J. Kilmartin (Berkeley: U of California P, 1999) 3, 43; and Modiano, "Avec Klarsfeld, contre l'oubli," *Libération* (2 November 1994), rpt. in *Patrick Modiano*, ed. M. Heck and R. Guidée (Paris: l'Herne, 2012) 178–86.

24. See "Correspondance Modiano/Klarsfeld" in *Patrick Modiano*, ed. Heck and Guidée, 147, 178–86.

25. On traces of Modiano's fiction-writing habits in *Dora Bruder*, see Alan Morris, "'Avec Klarsfeld, contre l'oubli': Patrick Modiano's *Dora Bruder*," *Journal of European Studies* 36/3 (2006): 269–93; Lynn A. Higgins, "Fugue States: Modiano Romancier," *Studies in 20th & 21st Century Literature* 31/2 (2007): 450–465.

Occupation's ethical disruptions and to make Ingrid's choice (which he had no right to imagine from within) seem like his own. Acceptance of limited, non-totalizing knowledge about Dora's mind demands that focalization remain external. Modiano/we cannot fuse with Dora, live in her psyche and skin, as Jean B. (Modiano alongside) had attempted to do with Ingrid.

In *Chien de printemps*, published the same year as *Dora Bruder*, Modiano confirms his retreat from the fusional model of earlier works. The intradiegetic narrator, self-appointed archivist of photographer Francis Jansen, half-heartedly revisits sites revealed in Jansen's photographs, but never tries to relive major parts of his mentor's life. Jansen is a man without a country: born in Belgium, an Italian citizen, a Jew obliged to live by fraud to escape deportation from his adoptive country, occupied France, and then, by 1964, life has passed him by. The traumatic final paragraphs, though, attest to Modiano's ability to renew his devices' strangeness. When Jansen contacts the Belgian consulate in Paris in 1964 to obtain a copy of his birth certificate, he receives documentation for his double, "a different Francis Jansen" born in Belgium in 1917, arrested in Rome in 1944, deported, "deceased in unknown place, unknown date."[26] This upsets Jansen's sense of identity: "a brother, a double died in our stead"; "his shadow ends up merging with us" (59). This feeling of overlay is perhaps what Modiano tried to convey through Jean B.'s vicarious identification with Ingrid's choice, but Jean B.'s effort to experience her Occupation is unlike *Chien de printemps*'s brutal execution-like ending. One Jansen escaped through no merit of his own, another Jansen died through no fault of his own. No implied author or autodiegetic narrator rights this absurd universe. *Chien de printemps*, mirroring *Dora Bruder*'s shift out of hegemonic narration, conveys the Shoah's aftereffects, but only as a shock arising not out of the plot's pairing of foreground with background—encounter between a young man and a photographer with a curious past—but surging from a random archive, which uncloaks an unknown *doppelgänger*'s death.

Étoile errante, on the other hand, reactivates an experiment Le Clézio began in his novel *Désert* (1980), which maps the psychic overlay of two characters, Lalla and Nour, through their very distinct immigration stories. In both novels, as Jean-Philippe Imbert remarks,

26. Modiano, *Suspended Sentences*, trans. Mark Polizzotti (New Haven: Yale University Press, 2015), 58. Translation of "Deceduto in luogo e data ignoti" is my own.

the intertwining of "two strands of narratives" (203) suggests an "overlap" or animistic exchange of souls between characters (206). But the attempt at identity fusion between Esther and Nejma begins in the aftermath of the Shoah and during the first Arab-Israeli war. These traumas or their sequels manifest themselves even in the novel's last scene, where Esther associates wartime Nice with Beirut under the Israeli invasion. The empathy that arises at the women's original meeting, and the notions that everyone has the right to live where she wishes in the sun's light (Nejma) or that amid conflicts one must cherish children's innocence (Esther), cannot sustain merger with the heartfelt Other. Le Clézio's initial answer to this dysfunction in later novels is to double down on fusion; other clashes with ideology and persecution are articulated with more nuance and pessimism, for example, in *Onitsha*, which narrates colonial employee Geoffroy Allen's mindmeld with legendary Umundri princes of Igboland, and *La quarantaine*, where modern narrator Léon absorbs the persona of his nineteenth-century familial namesake, the *other* Léon who disappeared forever among Mauritius's coolies.

In *Révolutions*, Le Clézio's experiments in overlay character- and era- mapping exhibit a more nuanced approach to the sympathy of minds. As Robert Decker asserts, "narrative plurality . . . reaches its apex" in this novel which "open[s] the narrative field to a plurality of voices with which the narrator fuses his own," creating a "shared narrative consciousness" and "interchangeable subjectivity."[27] Jean Marro, pondering his family history at the end of his wanderings, after saying "It has been so long ago," goes on to ask: "What has once been, can it exist once again? Can one live at the same time in several epochs?"[28] After the novel's midpoint, once Jean has revisited his blind spinster aunt Cathy Marro and realizes he can mimic her hypnotic soliloquies retelling the family's Mauritian roots but cannot absorb her inner vision, the narration's multi-voiced texture grows exponentially, allowing Jean to decathect and craft a future. Companion narrative voices, avatars of his mind that are outside the ken of his lived experience, proliferate and mix with events that he truly has experienced: immigration diaries of anti-slavery Breton founders of the family dynasty; Kilwa's words, daughter of the slave Kiambé

27. Robert Decker, "Polyphony and Recursive Memory in J. M. G. Le Clézio's Mauritian Novels," unpublished article (2015).

28. Le Clézio, *Révolutions* (Paris: Gallimard, 1997), 551, my translation.

who was the companion of Ratsitatane, *marron* rebel; youthful Cathy Marro's diary recounting the fateful end of her friendship with the girl Sopapramba and the exile of the narrator's branch of the Marro family in 1910; external rumors andechoes of the Algerian war that impel Jean's flight to London; and Jean's dialogues in Mexico City in 1968 with indigenous Pamela and her brother who flee political repression, inciting Jean's return to France and to his love, Mariam. There are no explicit signs that Jean narrates all the stories, yet his mind implicitly links voices from his atavistic past and transnational life, making an n-dimensional mental zone, which, says Marina Salles, "causes spatio-temporal limits of individual existence to shatter" (249, my translation). Voices, brought into proximity with Jean, define him as a nexus of, though not quite as a total fusion with, plural worlds. Nicholas Pien notes Le Clézio's quest since *Le procès-verbal* for "original harmony," fusion with the cosmos, but "writing alone can reunite spaces and times, mix them and make them *coincide*" (author's emphasis).[29] The harmony is convincing in *Révolutions*, but Esther's and Nejma's dialogisms or mind echoes are not strong enough to overcome their dissonances in *Étoile errante*.

In Modiano and Le Clézio, narrative strategies based on the assimilation or imagined fusion of otherwise distinct psyches reflect the desire to establish an ethical analogy between characters linked by genealogical atavism, moral affinity, or co-sympathetic psychic experience. But this desire for analogy, affinity, or metempsychosis does not motivate genocide and war. No moral order can be instilled in those who displace children to the camps. *Voyage de noces* and *Étoile errante* are absorbing, until a crisis point where the founding analogy between Jean B. and Ingrid, or Esther and Nejma, falls apart. *Voyage de noces* exposes limits of the empathetic merger of minds (of their imagined narrative fusion) as a way of confronting the Shoah, which only greater distance between the writer and Dora Bruder's story and a reduction of the narrator's hegemony can convey. Le Clézio, after *Étoile errante*, adopts a greater overlapping of one character's mind and thought with the with minds of sympathetic others, but he also shields focalizing characters from too frontal a contact with overt historical violence like the 1948 war. While *Révolutions* continues to debate the merits of enchanted attempts to merge with other minds

---

29. Nicolas Pien, *Le Clézio, la quête de l'accord originel* (Paris: L'Harmattan, 2004), 307.

and eras, protagonist Jean Marro espouses a chorus of consciousnesses without pretending to fuse his own mind with any of those other, disparate consciousnesses and identity positions. In espousal, as opposed to fusion, each partner retains difference and distinction. *Révolutions* replots *Étoile errante*'s abcissae and sets a variant path for Le Clézio's narratives. *Chien de printemps,* likewise, draws in novelistic terms the ethical lessons of *Dora Bruder* and shifts the paradigm of Modiano's earlier fusional fictions.

SUSAN RUBIN SULEIMAN

Humor, Parody, and the Quest for Jewish Identity in Modiano's *La place de l'étoile*

> Dr. Spielvogel, this is my life, my only life, and I'm living it in the middle of a Jewish joke! I am the son in the Jewish joke—*Only it ain't no joke!*
>
> —Philip Roth, *Portnoy's Complaint*

> Yiddish humor is cuttingly sharp; it contains more of harshness than merriment.
>
> —Ruth Wisse, *The Schlemiel as Modern Hero*

La place de l'étoile occupies a unique place in Modiano's oeuvre. Not only is it his first novel, published when he was not yet twenty-three years old and earning him instant fame in French letters, but it is also his only work that can be called humorous. *La place* is a very funny book, in an insolent, harsh, painful kind of way. Jean Cau, a now obscure but then well-known writer who prefaced the book in 1968, compared it to a "cat maddened by pain that leaps in your face and scratches you bloody." And he characterized the young author's voice as a "grand cri," a loud scream.[1] To readers who are familiar with the melancholy murmur of Modiano's later works, or even with the cool swing rhythms of his second novel, *La ronde de nuit* (which

---

1. Jean Cau, Preface to Modiano, *La place de l'étoile* (Paris: Gallimard, 1968), 3–5. Modiano deleted some passages, as well as Cau's preface, in reissues of the novel after 1968, some as early as the first Folio edition that dates from 1975. (For a detailed study of these changes, most of them minor, see Jacques Lecarme, "Quatre versions de *La place de l'étoile*," in *Modiano ou les intermittences de la mémoire*, ed. Anne-Yvonne Julien (Paris: Hermann, 2010), 103–109. In subsequent references, I will cite page numbers from the first Folio edition, in parentheses. Unless otherwise stated, all translations are my own.

YFS 133, *"Detecting" Patrick Modiano*, ed. Golsan and Higgins, © 2018 by Yale University.

58

is usually mentioned with *La place de l'étoile* and *Les boulevards de ceinture* as forming the "Occupation trilogy"), *La place de l'étoile* appears all the more anomalous—and interesting. Why did Modiano not continue in that vein? one wonders. Was it simply a case of youthful insolence, which he abandoned after indulging in it to his heart's content? Or did this book, by its very logic, lead to a conclusion that did not require (or even allow) further exploration down the same road?

"JEWISH JOKE"

The novel begins with an epigraph that is identified in parentheses as an "histoire juive," a Jewish joke:

> In the month of June 1942, a German officer approaches a young man and says to him: "Excuse me, sir, where is the Place de l'Étoile?" The young man points to the left side of his chest.
>
> —(Jewish joke)

Critics who have written about the novel sometimes mention this opening anecdote, which, despite its collective reference as a "Jewish joke," may have been invented by Modiano himself for the occasion. Curiously, however, none of the more than a dozen commentaries I have read has actually discussed the joke, or examined how it relates to what follows. Yet its prominent placing on its own page, in the very beginning of the book, surely invites our scrutiny. Like all good jokes, this one involves a reversal of expectations: instead of giving the officer the directions he needs to the famous tourist site, the young man points to his chest. And like many good jokes, this one depends on a verbal displacement, in fact two of them. The joke is in the slippage between two meanings of the word *place* in French: on the one hand, a geographical or topographical designation; on the other, a space large or small that an object or a person may occupy. Similarly with the word *étoile*, star: capitalized as part of the name of the most famous *place* in Paris, it is an obvious destination to which someone newly arrived in the city may ask directions. But as the object made of yellow cloth that was forcibly assigned to be worn by Jews in occupied France in June 1942 (note the careful mention of the date in the joke), the star becomes a marker of exclusion and persecution—very far from the pleasures of tourism. By pointing to the left side of his chest in answer to the officer's question, the young man designates himself as a Jew, one for whom the "place of the star" is a concrete bodily experience, not an abstract name. Furthermore, he does so to a German officer, who represents the very authority that has created this situation and thereby made the joke's word play possible.

Is the young man actually wearing a star, in this story? We are not told, and it doesn't matter all that much: either way, his gesture points to his own new status as a pariah—an outcast in relation to the German occupiers, but also in relation to his non-Jewish fellow Parisians. We know from many personal testimonies (including most recently from the diary of Hélène Berr, not published until 2009) how severe a blow it was to Jews in France, especially those who had been in the country for generations, to be marked by the star in the eyes of their fellow citizens. Personally, I think the joke is stronger if the young man is not wearing the star (at least, not yet), for in that case he appears as the agent of his own denunciation. The officer has not set him apart—he addresses him as Monsieur, as he would any Frenchman. It is the young man himself who, by pointing to his chest, denounces his status as a Jew.[2]

That gesture is why the joke is funny in a horrible kind of way, and pertinent to this novel: the pseudo-comic gesture of self-denunciation by a persecuted Jew will be repeated several times in the narrative that follows. But who exactly is being made fun of in this anecdote? Freud taught us that all jokes have an aggressive element: who then is being attacked here? Putting it another way, how should we interpret the young man's self-denunciation? One possible interpretation is that he is a fool, an innocent who, perhaps still stunned by this latest humiliation, points to what is henceforth the "place of the star" for him and other Jews in Paris. This kind of fool is also known as a *schlemiel*. According to the dictionary definition, the schlemiel is a guy who "handles a situation in the worst possible manner," or who "repeatedly brings bad luck on himself by his own ineptness."[3]

---

2. When I first presented this essay as a lecture at Columbia University, someone in the audience raised the possibility that the young man might not be a Jew, but rather a non-Jewish Frenchman who is playing around with the German soldier, perhaps manifesting resistance. This is indeed a possible interpretation, but I think a remote one that is less pertinent to Modiano's novel. As I explain, the epigraph foreshadows the painful humor of the narrative as a whole.

3. *Universal Jewish Encyclopedia*, quoted in Sanford Pinsker, *The Schlemiel as Metaphor: Studies in the Yiddish and American Jewish Novel* (Carbondale: Southern Illinois University Press, 1971), 5.

In popular parlance, he is the guy who's always spilling hot soup on himself, and on anyone luckless enough to be near him (the luckless guy is known as the schlemazl). There exist many versions of the schlemiel in Jewish folklore and literature, from the lovable failures and bumblers of Sholem Aleichem to Saul Bellow's exquisitely self-conscious and self-defeating intellectual, Herzog. But as Ruth Wisse points out in her book on the schlemiel as modern hero, this figure has another side as well: his "absolute defenselessness" may function on occasion as the only defense against brutal might. The schlemiel, in his most interesting incarnations, is a paradoxical figure embodying both weakness and strength. Wisse notes that in Jewish literature, he has been used as "the symbol of an entire people in its encounter with surrounding cultures and its opposition to their opposition."[4] In that light, we might interpret the young man's gesture not as a fool's mistake but as a provocation, an ironic, in-your-face assertion: "For you the Place de l'Étoile is a must-see tourist sight," his gesture may be telling the officer, "but for me it is my life, or very possibly my death. And by the way, I hope you appreciate my clever pun!" As both Freud and Wisse (in her more recent book, No Joke) have emphasized, self-deprecation is a hallmark of Jewish humor—which is one reason why it is so difficult for a non-Jew to tell a Jewish joke without sounding anti-Semitic. But in this particular joke, the young schlemiel is not only self-deprecating, he is downright self-destructive—at the very least, he is playing a version of Russian roulette, exposing himself to deathly danger. And for what? The price may be too high to pay, just to score a clever pun.

Before leaving this little joke behind, we must note just how deeply embedded it is in French language and history. Many jokes travel well ("Two Jews meet on a train . . ."), even if they refer to specific histories: "'If you were Hitler's child, what would be your greatest wish?' 'To be an orphan.'" (Fill in any other evil dictator's name for Hitler). But Modiano's joke needs extended explanations for non-French speakers, and even French speakers may need some help: to "get" the joke, one has to know what "June 1942" means in recent French history, specifically for Jews. And that's only the beginning.

4. Ruth Wisse, The Schlemiel as Modern Hero (Chicago: University of Chicago Press, 1971), 4.

SCHLEMILOVITCH, FATHER AND SON

The narrator of *La place de l'étoile* gives us his name on the very first page: Raphaël Schlemilovitch—which means literally "son of schlemiel." But Raphaël's father has the same last name: these two are clearly from a long line of schlemiels, each one already a "son of." The narrator's name immediately situates us on the terrain of satire, or of allegory, where proper names are signposts and transparent bearers of meaning. Raphaël Schlemilovitch is designated as a comic figure, flat as cardboard, from the moment he is named—but the fact that he is not a "realistic" character does not mean we should not take him seriously. Schlemilovitch's name is first mentioned by two unrepentant anti-Semites, "Léon Rabatête" and "docteur Bardamu," who write vicious articles about him after he has published a book that claims to unmask "Bardamu" as a Jew. Modiano has a terrific time here, lampooning the ideas as well as the style of two collaborationist writers who survived the war. "Rabatête," aka Lucien Rebatet, writes with his usual bluntness: "How much longer will we have to sit and watch the antics of Raphaël Schlemilovitch? How much longer will that Jew walk around flaunting his neuroses and his epilepsies? [. . .] How much longer will half-breeds like him go on insulting the sons of France?" As for "docteur Bardamu," aka Louis-Ferdinand Céline, he outdoes himself in the use of his signature exclamation marks and suspension points, as well as his obscenities and incomplete sentences: ". . . Schlemilovitch? . . . Ah, the mold of stinking ghetto, . . . swooning shithouse . . . fucking foreskin! . . . Lebanese . . . asswipe! . . . (13–14).

Judging by these perfectly tuned parodies of anti-Semitic writing, Modiano's Raphaël Schlemilovitch fits well into Wisse's characterization of the schlemiel as "the symbol of an entire people in its encounter with surrounding cultures." He also fits the second half of the definition: "and its [entire people's] opposition to its opposition." Unlike the traditional schlemiel, however, Modiano's Schlemilovitch is loud and vociferous, a combative young man who gives as good as he receives. If Dr. Bardamu is so angry at him, it's because he wrote a book titled *Bardamu démasqué*, in which he demonstrated that Bardamu was Jewish—indeed, that he was "the greatest Jewish writer of all times." That's why Bardamu writes so much about "the Jewish question," argues Schlemilovitch, and why he speaks about his "brothers in race" so passionately. In fact, Raphaël concludes,

"Only Jews can understand one of their own, only a Jew can speak knowledgeably about Dr. Bardamu" (16). It takes one to know one. With this hilarious reversal of Charles Maurras's famous dictum that only a "true Frenchman" can understand Racine, whose works will forever remain opaque to Jewish "foreigners," Modiano makes clear that his own intentions are to "oppose the opposition" of the surrounding culture toward Jews, and that he will do so by means of outrageous humor. Many years later, in *Dora Bruder*, Modiano explained—*sans* humor this time—how he came to write his first novel:

> [. . .] I had discovered among [my father's] books certain works by anti-Semitic writers of the forties, books that he had bought at the time, no doubt in order to try and understand what these people had against him. And I can imagine his surprise at the descriptions of that imaginary, fantasmatic monster whose threatening shadow ran along the walls, with his hooked nose and his claw-like hands, that creature rotten through and through by his vices [. . .] I wanted, in my first book, to respond to all those people whose insults had wounded me on account of my father. And, on the terrain of French prose, to shut them up once and for all.[5]

La place de l'étoile, according to this account, was a rescue effort by the son, written in order to avenge the insults suffered by the father—but also to make a place for the son himself "on the terrain of French prose." Shutting up the anti-Semites once and for all involved, among other stylistic choices, the use of a ferocious humor that beat the anti-Semites at their own game. Raphaël Schlemilovitch becomes, for a while—in his fantasy, that is—a Jewish anti-Semite and collaborator with the Nazis, friend of German Ambassador Otto Abetz and other Nazi dignitaries, whom a mere "juif honteux" (self-hating Jew) like André Maurois envies for his success. In a perceptive essay on the novel, Bruno Chaouat calls this a "homeopathic" cure for the poison of anti-Semitism, since Raphaël often sounds just like the writers that Modiano was trying to silence with his book.[6] One of

<hr/>

5. Patrick Modiano, *Dora Bruder* (Paris: Gallimard, 1997), 72–73. For the translation of this passage that follows, I consulted and significantly modified Joanna Kilmartin's version in English (University of California Press, 1999).

6. Bruno Chaouat, "*La place de l'étoile*, quarante ans après," in *Lectures de Modiano*, ed. Roger-Yves Roche (Nantes: Éditions Cécile Defaut, 2009), 110.

Raphaël's fantasies is that he dons an SS uniform and is killed on the Eastern front in 1944.

In the above paragraph from *Dora Bruder*, the father's cameo appearance is that of a schlemiel: Modiano surmises that in the 1940s, during a time when he was in mortal danger as a Jew trying to survive in Paris, his father went and bought the hateful writings of a Rebatet and a Céline "in order to try and understand what these people had against him." Only a schlemiel would do that. But as Modiano shows us in the longer sequence in which this paragraph appears, his actual father was no schlemiel: instead, Albert Modiano appears to have been an angry, brutal man who had survived the war in Paris by befriending some very unsavory people (supposedly he even worked for the Gestapo, though I have seen no documentation to prove that) and who, in 1963, had his 18-year old son arrested and taken to the police station as a "hoodlum" after the boy (sent by his mother) knocked on Albert's door to ask for the money he owed for child support. A few years later, Modiano *père* stole his son's military papers and sent them to the authorities, to try and have him forcibly enrolled in the army.[7]

Modiano never saw his father again after that last incident, he recounts in *Dora Bruder*. But in *La place de l'étoile*, he portrays Raphaël Schlemilovitch's father as a gentle soul, a constant wanderer and small-time crook who had survived the war in Paris through his wits and then emigrated to New York, where he started a business manufacturing kaleidoscopes that nobody bought. When Raphaël, newly enriched by his inheritance from a fabulously wealthy Venezuelan uncle, summons him to a visit with the promise of sharing his wealth, Schlemilovitch *père* flies in from New York, dressed in a "suit of Nile-blue wool, a green-striped shirt, a red tie, and Persian lamb shoes" (55). Thus attired in full schlemiel garb, he shares some moments of intimacy with his son—for example, they wander through Paris arm in arm, while the father, a great admirer of Céline's prose style, sings "fragments of *Bagatelles pour un massacre*," Céline's anti-Jewish diatribe, that he has learned by heart. (*Bagatelles*, first published in 1938, was reissued in occupied Paris in 1941, just in time to be bought by the Jew who wanted to find out what "those people" had against him). A few days later, when he accompanies

7. Modiano, *Dora Bruder*, 70–74.

Raphaël to Bordeaux (where the latter will enroll in a preparatory
course for the École Normale Supérieure, since that is the door to
assimilation in France, he believes), father and son engage in a comic
riff worthy of the Marx brothers, with an added dash of Beckett's Didi
and Gogo, the tramps of *Waiting for Godot*:

> In the taxi taking us to the Hotel Splendid, I whisper to my father:
> "The driver certainly belongs to the French Gestapo, you big lug.
> Your handsome Levantine mug has aroused his suspicion."
> "You think so? says my father, who is enjoying the game. That's
> very upsetting [. . .] At the first red light, we'll jump out."
> "Impossible, the doors are locked."
> "Then what?"
> "We wait. Without getting discouraged."
> "*Tout va très bien, madame la marquise.*"[Everything's fine, Ma-
> dame la Marquise]
> "We can always pretend we're Jewish collaborators. Sell them the
> Forest of Fontainebleau, cheap. I'll confess I used to work at *Je suis
> partout* [virulent anti-Semitic newspaper] before the war." (65)

We can almost imagine the two schlemiels shuffling in a vaudeville,
with the father actually breaking into song: "Tout va très bien, madame la marquise" was the refrain of a hit song of the 1930s, staging
a series of phone conversations between a traveling marquise and her
servants back home. The servants report one disaster after another at
the château, each one worse than the one before, but keep repeating
that "Everything's fine, Madame la marquise," to increasingly absurd
effect. The song was composed in 1935 by the Jewish musician Paul
Misraki, who fled France in 1940 and spent the war years in South
America; well before then, the refrain had acquired the meaning of
"blindness in the face of disaster," according to that indispensable research tool, Wikipedia (in this case, Wikipédia). Schlemilovitch *père*
quotes the line as part of the fantasy he elaborates with his son about
being arrested by the Gestapo, in 1960s Bordeaux! Theirs is just a
game, we are told ("il se prend au jeu")—but behind the game is the
serious possibility of what might have been, and what actually *was*
for many people in the real world during the war.

This is where we came in, isn't it? The combination of schlemiel-
hood and seriousness that characterizes the book's opening joke is
also to be found in the father and son vaudeville shtick. The self-
denunciation in the joke is itself reenacted with variations in two
separate episodes in the novel, featuring first the father and then the

son. The episode starring Schlemilovitch *père* is recounted as part of his life story, which Raphaël summarizes shortly after his father arrives from New York. Born in Caracas into a Sephardic Jewish family, the young Schlemilovitch *père* (we never find out his first name) had to "quickly leave America in order to escape from the police of the dictator of the Galapagos, whose daughter he had seduced" (shades of Albert Cohen's Solal, the eponymous hero of Cohen's first novel, published in 1930). In France, the handsome young Schlemilovitch *père* embarked on his brilliant if shady career by becoming secretary to the arch-swindler Stavisky; ten years later, his son tells us, a photo of him as a "dangerous character" was featured in the anti-Jewish exhibition at the palais Berlitz (earlier, Raphaël had already mentioned this infamous 1941 exhibition, purporting to show all the harm that Jews had done to and in France). We then come to the episode proper, a variant of the initial Jewish joke:

> My father was not lacking in humor: he had gone one afternoon to the palais Berlitz and offered to act as guide to a few militiamen.[8] When they stopped in front of his photo, he burst out: "Yoo-hoo, here I am." No doubt about it, Jews will do anything to call attention to themselves. (58)

As with the young man in the opening joke, we cannot be sure whether Schlemilovitch *père*, in this vignette, is an idiot or a daredevil playing Russian roulette. His son the narrator suggests the latter, but that may be simply because he himself can't resist a good punch line: with deadpan irony, Raphaël attributes his father's quasi-suicidal self-denunciation to his "typically Jewish" craving for attention!

Raphaël himself has a starring role in a later variant of the Jewish joke. During his visit to Vienna, where his mental state becomes increasingly deranged, Raphaël is stopped by a policeman who asks to see his papers. When he refuses to comply, the policeman arrests him—but Raphaël is convinced that the police station is headed by a

8. The Milice was an armed paramilitary force under Vichy, founded by Joseph Darnand and composed mainly of young thugs, whose mission was to hunt Jews and *résistants*. Modiano committed an anachronism, however, in referring to *miliciens* in 1941: the Milice was not founded until January 1943. In editions of *La place de l'étoile* after 1975, the word *milicien* is replaced by "touristes," which is less dramatic but more accurate historically.

Nazi officer. The whole scene has a burlesque quality, starting with the quote of a famous line by Verlaine:

> When I entered his office, the police chief, a cultivated S.S. who had read the French poets, asked me:
> "You there, what have you done with your youth?" [from Verlaine's poem "Le ciel est par-dessus le toit"]
>   I explained to him how I had ruined it. And then I told him about my impatience: at the age when others prepare for their future, my only thought was to sabotage myself. There was the time, for example, at the gare de Lyon, under the German occupation. I was supposed to take a train that would carry me away, far from misery and anxiety. Travelers were lined up near the ticket counter. All I had to do was wait half an hour to get a ticket. But no, I climbed aboard a first-class carriage, without a ticket, like an impostor. When the German guards came to the compartment, at Chalon-sur-Saône, they arrested me. I didn't resist. I told them that despite my false papers in the name of Jean Cassis de Coudray-Macouard, I was a JEW. What a relief! (172–73)

The self-destructive aspect of the initial joke is here carried even further: Raphaël breathes a sigh of relief after sabotaging himself. The name on his false papers, incidentally, is the same as the one his father had had on *his* false papers, mentioned a hundred pages earlier. A few pages before this episode, Raphaël had stated, "a Jew does not have the right to commit suicide. He must leave that luxury to Werther." But he can invite being killed by others, it would seem. Raphaël is not killed for being Jewish, despite his best efforts: he was born too late for that, the Viennese police chief tells him. "If you had been born earlier, I would have sent you to Auschwitz [. . .]. But now we live in more civilized times" (173–74) He gives Raphael a plane ticket to Tel Aviv instead.

SIEGFRIED, GÜNTHER, HERMANN . . . LEVY

The last major sequence in the novel, recounting Raphaël's visit to Israel, is generally deemed to be a problem for interpreters. Right after he arrives in Tel-Aviv, Raphael is arrested by Israeli security police for being a "French Jew," a neurotic weakling who reads Proust and Kafka and for whom the blond sabras have no use. They throw him in jail and then send him, along with several other European Jews, to a kibbutz concentration camp, where he will be either reeducated or killed. The narrative becomes more and more phantasmagorical in this sequence, as Raphaël hallucinates that the Israeli jail (which is itself a fantasy) is a Gestapo torture chamber in Paris during the war. In his deranged view, the Israeli torturers have German first names (Siegfried, Günther, Hermann), and the interrogating officers all resemble notorious Nazis.

The equation of Israel with Nazi Germany has become a familiar trope in anti-Israeli discourses in recent years. Modiano's evocation of it in *La place de l'étoile* has made some readers extremely uneasy: Was the author espousing the strongly anti-Israel turn of French left-wing intellectuals after the 1967 war? That could be a logical conclusion, given the French political context at the time the novel appeared. But it would be wrong. Raphaël's hallucinatory view of Israeli society is not a post-1967 indictment of Israel's oppressive policy toward Arabs—Arabs are not even mentioned in this sequence, nor is the 1967 war. If Raphaël equates the Israeli authorities with Nazis, it's because he sees Nazis everywhere. In fact, his world seems to be divided into only two categories of people: Jews and Nazis, or if not Nazis, then virulent anti-Semites. The opening gambit parodying Rebatet and Céline is followed by other episodes set in the provinces, where the local population hates Jews without ever having met one. The twist in the Israeli sequence is that these two categories become fused: even some Jews can act like Nazis, if the circumstances are right. Unlike the Nazis, however, the Israeli interrogators despise Raphaël Schlemilovitch not because he is a Jew, but because he is a weak and "neurotic" Jew, the embodiment of the diasporic schlemiel. The general who, in Raphaël's eyes, looks just like Joseph Darnand, founder of the murderous Milice under Vichy, expresses nothing but scorn for "Jewish anxiety, Jewish lament, Jewish anguish, Jewish despair." He therefore spits on all of Raphaël's heroes, from Proust and Kafka to Charlie Chaplin, the Marx brothers, and the tubercular painter Modigliani (whom Raphaël calls his Italian cousin).

But what is a Jew, exactly? That is the question that Raphaël Schlemilovitch struggles with from one end of the novel to the other. He tries on identities like a series of costumes: the anti-Semitic Jew, the collaborationist Jew, the Jewish gangster, the "distinguished" Jew, the snobbish Jew—and through it all, the self-conscious Jew who can never stop being aware of his status as "other," not even in the Jewish homeland. At key moments, Raphaël's narrative slips from first to third to second person pronouns, splitting his identity into pieces like the kaleidoscopes manufactured by his father, which produce only shattered views of the human face.

In terms of narrative logic, the Israeli episode is simply the culmination of Raphaël's failed quest for a livable Jewish identity. In the end, he finds himself back in Vienna, in a hospital room where Dr. Freud receives him with the reassuring message that "the Jew does not exist," as "Jean-Paul Schweitzer de la Sarthe" has shown; therefore he should stop worrying and read Sarthe's "penetrating essay," *Réflexions sur la question juive*. Modiano is here lampooning Sartre's famous definition of the Jew as "one whom others call Jew," implying that Jewishness as an identity has no positive content. But despite Dr. Freud's advice, Raphaël is not reassured—on the contrary, he insists that he will accept only Dr. Bardamu as his therapist. He does not say why, but we can surmise that it's because Bardamu, at least, believes that Jews exist! As for Raphael Schlemilovitch, he is tired.

Portnoy, at the end of his Complaint, is told by his analyst that "now vee may perhaps to begin." Raphaël Schlemilovitch ends up in a less hopeful place—his tiredness signals the end of a road, not a new beginning. But Modiano, for his part, may have found a way out. After *La place de l'étoile*, he would never again write about a specifically *Jewish* quest for identity. His heroes become more generalized, and if they are Jewish their Jewishness is only implied, not explicitly mentioned. When he does return to Jews, in *Dora Bruder*, it is as an empathetic witness to their suffering, not as a Jew himself. Modiano tells us in that book that as a young man he had wanted to avenge the insults suffered by his father, and to silence the anti-Semitic writers once and for all by his own words. But right after that, he adds: "Today I am aware of the childish naiveté of that project; most of those writers were gone: condemned to death, exiled, demented or dead of old age. Yes, unfortunately I was too late."[9] In fact, in terms of French literary history, and of French history *tout court*, *La place de l'étoile* was early rather than late. Before *The Sorrow and the Pity*, before Lanzmann's *Shoah*, before the "obsession with Jewish memory" that would become a feature of French intellectual life from the 1970s on,

9. *Dora Bruder*, 73.

Modiano[10] found a way to bring the question of Jewish identity into the limelight—and to earn for himself a lasting place on the "terrain of French prose."

10. A precursor who is often mentioned in discussions of *La place de l'étoile* is Bernard Frank, whose *Géographie universelle* (1953) and *Israël* (1955) display a similar talent for provocation and self-invention, as well as a similar obsession with Jewish identity. I don't find these books nearly as accomplished as *La place de l'étoile*, however. Frank, born in 1929 into an established French Jewish family, survived the war in hiding with his parents. Like Modiano, he reached literary renown while still in his twenties; he published several novels as well as nonfiction works (the two books above are called *essais*) and journalism, but his early promise was not fully realized. He died in 2006.

GERALD PRINCE

Improper Nouns: Patrick Modiano's *Rue des boutiques obscures*

The importance of proper names for Patrick Modiano and in his work is well known.[1] The title of his first novel, *La place de l'étoile*, no doubt evokes many things: the yellow star (*étoile*) that Jews had to wear under the Occupation and that the novelist's Jewish father never wore; the destiny of his Flemish mother, who was an actress but, perhaps because of World War II, never became a star; the stardom that he himself may have aspired to (and later achieved); the good or bad luck that is thought to preside over one's life; the place of the heart behind the yellow star, and so on.[2] But it also designates the Parisian square around the Arc de Triomphe, now officially called "Place Charles de Gaulle," not far from the headquarters of the French Gestapo on rue Lauriston. Similarly, the title of what is arguably Modiano's most famous work—*Dora Bruder*—consists of a name, one that may call to his readers' mind the pseudonym Freud gave the rebellious and aphonic Ida Bauer or the concentration camp (Dora-Mittelbau) established

1. See, for example, Didier Blonde, "L'abonné absent," in *Patrick Modiano*, ed. Raphaëlle Guidée and Maryline Heck (Paris: L'Herne, 2012), 78–80; Stéphane Chaudier, "Pourquoi mentir," *Le magazine littéraire*, Hors-Série-no. 2 (October 2014): 46–49; Tiphaine Samoyault, "Mélancolie blanche," *Le magazine littéraire*, 58–59; and Tiphaine Samoyault, "Le nom propre," in *Patrick Modiano*, ed. Guidée and Heck, 86–89. On Modiano, see Bruno Blanckeman, *Lire Patrick Modiano* (Paris: Armand Colin, 2009); Dervila Cooke, *Present Pasts: Patrick Modiano's (Auto)Biographical Fictions* (Amsterdam-New York: Rodopi, 2005); Denis Cosnard, *Dans la peau de Patrick Modiano* (Paris: Fayard, 2010); Paul Gellings, *Poésie et mythe dans l'œuvre de Patrick Modiano. Le fardeau du monde* (Paris-Caen: Lettres Modernes Minard, 2000); Alan Morris, *Patrick Modiano* (Oxford-Washington: Berg, 1996); and Colin Nettelbeck and Penelope Hueston, *Patrick Modiano: Pièces d'identité. Écrire l'entretemps* (Paris: Minard, coll. Archives des lettres modernes, 1986).

2. On the writer's family origins, see, in particular, Patrick Modiano, *Un pedigree* (Paris: Gallimard, 2004), 9–14.

YFS 133, *"Detecting" Patrick Modiano*, ed. Golsan and Higgins, © 2018 by Yale University.

in 1943 near Buchenwald. Perhaps it also conjures Modiano's father's cousin Dora, whose three brothers were murdered by the SS in September 1943, and, certainly, it conjures Modiano's brother (*Bruder*) Rudy, whose death in 1957 at the age of ten proved traumatic for Patrick and to whom he dedicated his first eight novels.[3]

A number of Modiano's other works, too, have a proper name for a title: *Villa triste* ("Sad Villa"), which, among other things, is the name used for various Italian locales where the Fascists held and tortured their prisoners; *Memory Lane*, which is the name of a song ("Memory Lane / Only once do horses go down Memory Lane / But the traces of their hooves still remain"); or *La petite bijou* (Little Jewel), a nickname given to the disconsolate narrator when she was child and a budding actress, before she was abandoned by her mother (herself a failed actress). Modiano's most explicitly autobiographical work—*Un pedigree*—not only gestures through its title toward a long series of names but it also sheds a good deal of light on many of them. Last but by no means least, the title of the novel to which much of what follows is devoted—*Rue des boutiques obscures*—refers to a street in Rome where the seat of the Communist party was located, at the edge of the old Jewish ghetto.[4] It can make one think of the fact that Rome was the capital of Fascist Italy, of the Italian origins of Modiano's father, and of small and dark ghetto shops. Perhaps too, because of the dreamlike quality of the novel, it evokes a (Jewish) writer as well as expert onomast whom Modiano admires: Georges Perec and his *La boutique obscure* (1973), which records one hundred and twenty-four dreams.

Furthermore, names abound in the body of Modiano's texts. For example, there are about one hundred names of persons, two hundred place names, and forty names of other entities in *Rue des boutiques obscures*. Chapter XIV of the novel is largely made up of the names of members of Latin American embassies and Chapter XIX consists solely of a name, an address, and a telephone number:

---

3. See Cosnard, *Dans la peau de Patrick Modiano*, 220.
4. All my references to this novel are to Modiano, *Missing Person*, trans. Daniel Weissbort (Boston: David R. Godine, 2005). Page numbers are indicated in the text. However, I use the title of the original version of the work—Patrick Modiano, *Rue des boutiques obscures* (Paris: Gallimard, 1978)—and I have kept the French spellings of all proper names.

"[Mansoure.] Jean-Michel. 1, rue Gabrielle, XVIIIᵉ. CLI 72–01" (92).[5] In general, Modiano likes mixing real names with fictional ones, which accentuates the oneiric character of his work: Georges Rollner with Sessue Hayakawa, say, Pulli with Chmara ("bad name" in Hebrew), Oleg de Wrédé, Freddie Howard de Luz, or Pedro McEvoy with Porfirio Rubirosa, Alec Scouffi, and Hoyningen-Huene. As many of the latter indicate, Modiano also shows a penchant for extravagant, theatrical, "foreign"-sounding names, which contrast, sometimes explicitly, with Franco-French names like Quintard or Picard, Hattier-Morel or Sergent-Delval, Denise Coudreuse or Guy Roland, and which connote otherness, displacement, exile, hybridity. Sometimes, the hybridity results from the conjunction of a Flemish (maternal) component and a Judeo-Mediterranean (paternal) one, as in Chalva Deyckecaire, Aldo Eykerling, or Choura Vervekken. Sometimes, a similar mixture can be found in a single name. Deyckecaire, Dekker, and Dekkers are all Flemish names, but they each evoke "Caire," Cairo, Egypt.[6] To escape the curse of origins, the vise of social constraints, the weight of the past, many characters adopt new names. Marc Newman becomes Gérard Valvert. Jean Dekker turns into Ambrose Guise (a telling surname). Raphaël Schlemilovitch (son of Schlemiel) acquires no fewer than three new monikers: Jean-François des Essarts, Jean Cassis de Coudray-Macouard, and Raphaël de Château-Chinon. In *Livret de famille*, uncle Alex, who worries about not looking French enough, introduces himself as François Aubert; and the narrator's father, Aldo, gets married under the name of Guy Jaspaard de Jonghe.

When Patrick Modiano asked his paternal uncle, Ralph, why he used "Gérin" as a name for the company he ran ("Établissements Gérin"), Ralph answered, with his unmistakably Parisian accent, that Italian-sounding names were not well regarded after the war. Similarly, Modiano's father used the name of his friend Henry Lagroua and several other names as well during the Occupation. The novelist himself was born *Jean* Patrick Modiano but preferred "Patrick" as a first name and considered using the shared pseudonym of "Hugues Stern" (*star*) for the songs he wrote with Hughes de Courson; he was

5. The English version mistakenly translates "Mansoure" as "Mr." See Modiano, *Missing Person*, 92 and Modiano, *Rue des boutiques obscures*, 136.
6. Born in Salonica, Modiano's paternal grandfather lived in Egypt for a while.

self-conscious about his last name and the Jewish origins it possibly concealed (or revealed).[7]

Modiano has often commented on names explicitly, pointing to their evocative power and the emotions they can provoke, referring to their function as a springboard for his imagination and a scaffolding for his work, discussing his use of them as a kind of call to various people who vanished, noting that they frequently constitute the only trace left of a person, and stressing the necessity and obligation of saving them from oblivion.[8] Many of his narrators and characters are similarly sensitive to them. In *Rue des boutiques obscures*, there are not only many names; there are also about fifty onomastic comments by various characters and, of course, by Guy Roland who, after all, is a character in search of a name. Some of these comments echo what Modiano said in interviews or other non-fictional texts (1–2, 109, 118) and some bring out the hybridity of certain names or their ordinariness, the protagonist's puzzlement about the name of various entities, or his perplexity regarding his own real name (41, 122, 158). Notable is the interest shown in the sonority of names. "Sonachitzé," for instance, sounds like "wind rustling in the trees" (23). Russian or Georgian names such as Troubetskoï, Orbeliani, Eristoff, Tchavatchavadzé are brilliant like the sound of cymbals, or muffled and mournful (26). "Waldo Blunt" is inflated like a balloon (46). "Portugal" is said to evoke the ocean, the sun, an orange drink, a beach umbrella (116). "Hoyningen-Huene" seems plaintive and "Oleg de Wrédé" pallid whereas "Rubirosa" is crimson and sparkling (96, 208).

Though many of the connotations and most of the denotations of the proper names in *Rue des boutiques obscures* have been identified and discussed, a few more probably deserve a mention. For example, Henriette Bogaerts, Denise Coudreuse's mother in the novel, points not only to the author's Flemish origins but also to his father's ancestry, since "Henriette" is the first name of Modiano's paternal grandmother, Henriette Lévy. At least ten or twelve of the embassy employees listed in chapter XIV—Gustavo J. Henriquez, say, Bienvenido Carrasco, Carlo Aristimuno Coll, Ismael Gonzalez Arevalo—

---

7. See Modiano, *Un pedigree*, 21 and 66; Cosnard, *Dans la peau de Patrick Modiano*, 11, 42, and 51.

8. See, for instance, Modiano, *Un pedigree*, 13. See also, Modiano, *Dora Bruder* (Paris: Gallimard, 1997), 85–86; François Busnel and Modiano, "L'entretien," *Lire* 430 (November 2014): 57 and 58; Heck and Modiano, "J'aurais pu croire que la boucle était bouclée, mais . . . ," *Le magazine littéraire*, 42–43.

are historical characters. R.L. de Oliveira Cezar, the diplomat who apparently certified that the Salonika archives were destroyed in a fire (66–67), was, in fact, the Argentinian Consul General in Paris and helped Jews and non-Jews during the Occupation. (He wrote an interesting novel set in Occupied France, *Hombres 40 Caballos 8*.) If Denise Coudreuse is a fictional character, both her first and last names have a number of Modianesque resonances. Apart from being the name of the young woman with whom the narrator of *Livret de famille* is in love, "Denise" is the name of Henri Lagroua's friend. "Coudreuse," which, in *Livret de famille*, is said to be the last name of André Bourlagoff's French governess, is characterized in *Villa triste* as a suave French moniker.[9] Hutte, the good father figure who gives the amnesic Guy Roland his new identity, appropriately bears a name meaning "small house" or "shelter." Finally, to my untrained ears, McEvoy, one of the protagonist's possible surnames, sounds a lot like "Ma che voi?" ("But who you?" in Italian) or "Ma che vuoi?" ("What do you want?" My name!)

Just as suggestive are the names of the songs appearing in the novel. For instance, *Sur les quais du vieux Paris* ("On the Piers of Old Paris"), which boasts a nostalgic title, was written by Ralph Erwin, a Jewish Austrian composer whose real name was Erwin Vogl and who was murdered in a French prison camp in 1943. *Sag Warum* ("Tell Me Why") was composed by Camillo Felgen, a Luxemberger who worked as a translator for the German occupiers.[10] Its lyrics are telling: "Sag warum existier ich in Schmerz und Angst?" ("Tell me why I exist in pain and fear?"). *El Reloj* ("The Clock"), which Rubirosa liked to play on the guitar, proves quite eloquent too —"Reloj no marques las horas . . . Reloj detén tu camino . . . Detén el tiempo en tus manos" ("Clock, do not mark the hours . . . Clock, stop your journey . . . Stop time in your hands")—as does *Tu me acostumbraste* ("You Got Me Used to"), Rubirosa's favorite song: "Tu me acostumbraste a todas esas cosas / Y tu me enseñaste que son maravillosas . . . / Porque no me enseñaste como se vive sin tí?" ("You got me used to all those things / And you taught me that they are marvelous . . . / Why didn't you teach me how to live without you?"). *Que reste-t-il*

9. See Modiano, *Livret de famille* (Paris: Gallimard, 1977), 77 and Modiano, *Villa triste* (Paris: Gallimard, 1975), 22.

10. Modiano's mother worked in the dubbing department of Continental Films, the German-controlled French film company in Occupied France.

de nos amours! ("What Is Left of Our Love?"), which was composed by Charles Trenet—who also wrote *Swing Troubadour*, the song that gives its name to the protagonist of *La ronde de nuit* (*Night Rounds*)—is full of wistfulness. As for *Auprès de ma blonde* ("Near to my blonde lass"), which was originally called (in the seventeenth century) *Le prisonnier de Hollande* ("The Prisoner from Holland"), it is also the title of a play by Marcel Achard in which Modiano's mother—a blonde, like Denise Coudreuse—had a small part.

Among the various figures, motifs, and themes with which names in *Rue des boutiques obscures* are associated, an obvious and prominent one is that of Oedipus, whose fate is inextricably tied with naming, sense, and reference. Think, for example, of "Oedipus killed Laios" versus "Oedipus killed his father," or of "Oedipus did not know that he married his mother" as opposed to "Oedipus did not know that he married Jocasta." Now, *Rue des boutiques obscures* is a kind of detective story, and its protagonists have been convincingly tied to Modiano's father, Modiano's mother, and Modiano himself.[11] For instance, Guy Roland—a detective, like Oedipus, and in a labyrinth, like Theseus who is also involved in his own father's death—may really be Pedro McEvoy, whose initials are the same as the author's and whose last name is that of an associate of Albert Modiano, Freddie McEvoy. Pedro is supposedly a Dominican subject employed by his country's embassy in Paris and Albert Modiano supposedly looked Latin American.[12] Moreover, Pedro McEvoy may really be Jimmy Pedro Stern, who marries Denise Coudreuse, a model working under the name of Muth (Mutter? Mother?), just like Freddie McEvoy married the French fashion model Claude Stéphanie Filatre and Albert Modiano married Louisa Colpijn who worked as a model for a while.

Another mythical story evoked by the novel's characters and onomastic features is the *Odyssey*. If Telemachus says to Athena, "My mother . . . tells me I am son to Odysseus, but it is a wise child that knows its own father," Guy Roland, who is "baptized" by Hutte, has a similarly problematic relation to the Name (or the Nay) of the Father.[13] If Odysseus is Noman, has several pseudonyms (Outis, Aethon,

11. See, for example, Cosnard, *Dans la peau de Patrick Modiano*, 151–64.

12. See Modiano, *Un pedigree*, 21.

13. Homer, *The Odyssey*, trans. Samuel Butler (New York: Race Point Publishing, 2015), 7.

Eperitus) and wanders for years before getting home, Guy Roland twice remarks that he is "nothing" (1, 84), may have gone by the name of Pedro McEvoy and/or by that of Jimmy Pedro Stern before his amnesia, and not only wanders through the streets of Paris and its environs but goes to Jouy-en-Josas, Vichy, Megève, as far as the island of Padipi, and, in order possibly to reach home, has "to return to [his] old address in Rome" (167).

Along with his wandering and his possible pseudonyms, the fact that Guy Roland may have been named Stern, may have lived at the edge of the Jewish ghetto in Rome, and may have tried to escape from Occupied France to go to Switzerland calls to mind the concern that Jews have shown for names, beginning with the Bible: Adam getting the power to name every living creature, Abram becoming Abraham, and Jacob being renamed Israel after wrestling with the angel. Besides, it calls to mind the tradition of onomastic Jewish jokes. Here is an old one: "A Jew goes to the state court and changes his name from Shulevitch to Smith. A week later he goes back to the court and wants to change his name to Jones. The judge says: 'Weren't you here last week? Didn't you change your name from Shulevitch to Smith? What's going on?' 'Oh! it's very simple. Now if they ask me "But what was your name before it was Jones, I'll say Smith.'" There is another old joke about how Chaim Shmendrick became Sean Ferguson. But "schoyn vergessen."

Just as they point to origin and buttress mythic subtexts, names in *Rue des boutiques obscures* help to bring out the metafictional dimension of Modiano's novel. Modiano never showed much affection or admiration for the New Novel, the New New Novel, the textual novel, or the Roman Tel Quel. From his perspective, the members of the Tel Quel group were "Martians"; he thought that the Nouveau Roman was "toneless and lifeless"; and he said: "Literature for literature's sake, research into writing, all this Byzantinism for professors and colloquia does not interest me."[14] Indeed, he is known for his readability and his "petite musique." But Modiano is also an avid reader. He's a fine pasticheur and practitioner of "la manière deux." He likes Céline, Queneau, and Perec. With his tortuous spaces, hazy

14. See Josane Duranteau, "L'obsession de l'anti-héros," *Le monde* (November 11, 1972), 13; Jean Montalbetti, "La haine des professeurs: Instantané Patrick Modiano," *Les nouvelles littéraires* (June 13, 1968): 2; Jean-Louis Ezine, "Sur la sellette: Patrick Modiano ou le passé antérieur," *Les nouvelles littéraires* (October 6, 1975): 5.

temporalities, uncertain investigations, hesitant narrations, he is perhaps not as far from the New Novelists as he claims. Not only has he sometimes been associated with the postmodern, but *Rue des boutiques obscures* in particular, which is a novel about anguish, loss, memory, and identity, can be read as a reflection on narrative and fiction.[15]

The novel is a kind of detective story, like Robbe-Grillet's *Les gommes*, and its protagonist is lost in a maze like the protagonist of Robbe-Grillet's *Dans le labyrynthe. Rue des boutiques obscures* multiplies the clichés of the genre (a bout with amnesia, good leads that prove to be bad ones, important but unlocatable witnesses) and it underlines the coincidences that allow for its development instead of trying to conceal them. Guy Roland unexpectedly meets André Wildmer in the wine-bar-cum-grocery just opposite his old detective agency, for example; Gay Orlow and Freddie Howard de Luz marry in the church in Nice that Hutte used to attend; and Freddie disappears from Tahiti a few days before the protagonist gets there. Early in the novel, Jean Heurteur even tells Guy Roland that "[t]here certainly are some strange coincidences" (12), and Guy later remarks: "Sometimes there are the oddest coincidences" (126).[16] The novel also contains several contradictions that accentuate its hazy, implausible, and even illogical temporality. For instance, Marie de Resen dies on October 25 and is buried on November 4. Ninth Day Divine Service is held on November 5. That day, Guy Roland meets Stioppa who shows him pictures of Gay Orlow, which leads him to write to Jean-Pierre Bernardy and ask for information about her. The answer he gets is dated October 23, 1965. Has a year (or more) gone by or is time out of joint? Similarly, Alec Scouffi, the historical author of *Au Poiss' d'Or, hôtel meublé* ("At the Golden Fish Residential Hotel") and *Navire à l'ancre* ("Ship at Anchor"), was murdered in 1932.[17] According to the novel, Denise Coudreuse lived in the same building as Scouffi (97, rue de

15. See Jeanne C. Ewert, "Lost in the Hermeneutic Funhouse: Patrick Modiano's Postmodern Detective," in *The Cunning Craft: Original Essays on Detective Fiction and Literary Theory,* ed. Ronald G. Walker and June M. Frazer (Macomb: Western Illinois Press, 1990), 166–73. On *Rue des boutiques obscures,* see also Cooke, *Present Pasts,* 178–92; Morris, *Patrick Modiano,* 80–88; and Gerald Prince, *Narrative as Theme: Studies in French Fiction* (Lincoln: University of Nebraska Press, 1992), 121–32.

16. See Cooke, *Present Pasts,* 182–83 and Morris, *Patrick Modiano,* 86.

17. In the novel, Scouffi is identified as the author of *Au Poisson d'or hôtel meublé* (155).

Rome) and Guy Roland or, rather, Pedro McEvoy, who was dating her at the time, is said to have passed him several times as he went up to her apartment. But, in 1932, Denise would have been no older than fifteen.

As already noted, Guy Roland is himself a detective. He enjoys reading detective stories—*Charlie Chan*, for example, with its foreign protagonist bearing a hybrid name, or *Lettres anonymes* ("Anonymous Letters"), published in 1942 and signed "François Sturel," the same name as that of the protagonist of Maurice Barrès' *Les déracinés* ("The Uprooted"). He also reads memoirs and he notices, in the bookcase of the Hotel Castille, Louis de Viel-Castel's *Histoire de la Restauration* ("History of the Restoration"). Guy is looking for his life or, at least, for a story that he can enter and find a place in. But even when he finds a story that may possibly fit him, it is never quite confirmed as his, since documents turn out to be semiotically indeterminate, human witnesses often prove forgetful or unreliable, new details can come to the surface and bring new light ("there was one last thing I would have to try: to return to my old address in Rome," 251), and new connections can always be established, including the ones pointed to in four different chapters told by a heterodiegetic narrator whose interventions undermine the realism of Modiano's text.[18] At the very beginning of the novel, like in every novel and, more particularly, like in Raymond Queneau's *Le chiendent*, the protagonist is nothing: "I am nothing. Nothing but a pale shape, silhouetted that evening against the café terrace, waiting for the rain to stop" (1). Soon, his name is mentioned and it will serve as a symbol for an increasingly large number of semes or propositions and function as a link to other names, other symbols, other stories: "waves passed through me, sometimes faint, sometimes stronger, and all these scattered echoes afloat in the air crystallized and there I was" (84).

The name Guy Roland is fictional. Along with an ID and a passport, it was given to the amnesia-stricken protagonist by his boss. Perhaps his real name was Pedro McEvoy. But that name too seems to be a fiction used as a cover for the Salonika born Jimmy Pedro Stern, whose own name (and story) may also be a fiction made possible by the destruction of the Salonikan archives. Other names, like Freddie Howard de Luz, similarly smack of fiction, not only because

18. See chapters 26, 32, 34, and 43.

they represent a story that the protagonist tries to slip into but also because they sound so improbable—"half English . . . half French . . . or Spanish," as Waldo Blunt says (41). Finally, that address in Rome itself conjures a fictional space.

Now, Rue des boutiques obscures is not the only place name in the novel that proves evocative. For instance, the appropriately named Garage de la Comète (Comet Garage) closed in 1952 "and is shortly to be replaced by a residential development" (106). The Collège de Luiza et d'Albany (Luiza and Albany School) calls to mind the first name of Modiano's mother and, perhaps, that of his father *Alb*ert too (135).[19] The "Café de la Restauration" was, indeed, the name of a café in Vichy (134). There is a restaurant called "L'équipe" in Megève (150). The Croix du Sud (Southern Cross), the name of the chalet in Megève where Guy Roland and Denise Coudreuse seek refuge, is also the name of a constellation of stars (147) as well as that of a pink diamond that Modiano's father had once bought, and rue Vital (1), the first street mentioned in the body of the text, is the street where Leo Israelowicz lived (he was the liaison officer of the U.G.I.F., the Union Générale des Israélites de France; accused of having helped the Gestapo; he was assassinated by a kapo in Auschwitz). But the Rue des boutiques obscures is special. It is not to be found, at least not in Rome. There one finds the via delle Botteghe Oscure.[20] If Modiano resorts to a French and non-existent name, perhaps it is to suggest that Guy Roland's identity—like that of us all—can only ever be found in some kind of fiction.

19. See Cosnard, *Dans la peau de Patrick Modiano*, 105.
20. The English version of the novel uses that Italian name (120, 167).

VANESSA DORIOTT ANDERSON

Mapping Modiano's Bordeaux

Paris is not Bordeaux, you know.

—Patrick Modiano, *La place de l'étoile*

It begins with a name. Patrick Modiano's narrators are distinctive for their very lack of distinction; among other shared characteristics is their fondness for the use of a pseudonym that reveals as much as it conceals of their identity. "Serge Alexandre" and "Guy Roland" are two examples of a naming ritual that evacuates the father's identity by replacing a foreign-sounding family name with two traditional French first names. This turn toward French authenticity simultaneously communicates the narrators' rootlessness, their lack of identity, and the geographical void that accompanies that lack. The name *Bordeaux* has a similar "authentic" French appeal that relies on its transformation from its precursor, Burdigala. The origins and meaning of Burdigala remain speculative. Phonically, a French speaker might well hear *bord d'eaux* in the city's name and associate it with its geographical proximity to the Garonne or the Atlantic, both meaningful sites of contact in the city's history. Thus the city's name is allusive and misleading, meaningful and mysterious. It refers back to its history, but that history is opaque. It gestures toward its geography, but that gesture is constructed. And over time, its name has lost its specificity, even its quality as a proper name, through its extension to a wine-producing region, the type of wine produced in that region, and the typical color of that wine.[1] It is a name, then, that conveys place while exceeding it, a contradictory name that encompasses provincial rootedness as well as cosmopolitan cultural consumption. As such, it is a name that encapsulates, in miniature, Modiano's literary

---

1. For a discussion of the ways in which Bordeaux's wine-producing economy promotes and relies on the construction of individual, commercial, and geographical reputations, see Pierre-Marie Chauvin, *Le marché des réputations: Une sociologie du monde des vins de Bordeaux* (Bordeaux: Éditions Féret, 2010).

YFS 133, *"Detecting" Patrick Modiano*, ed. Golsan and Higgins, © 2018 by Yale University.

81

universe, and it is fitting that it constitutes a complicated, contradictory geographical, historical, and cultural site within Modiano's body
of work.

Critical interest in Modiano's approach to geography, and more
specifically, urban topography, has grown in the past decade. As Paul
Gellings has observed, "In Patrick Modiano's writing, the space that
takes shape carries forth the narrative."[2] While the majority of contributions to the spatial study of Modiano's novels rightly situate Paris at
the physical and emotional center of his body of work, key secondary
sites are increasingly acknowledged for their place in the constellation of real spaces that underpin the Modianosphere. Indeed, this in-
terplay between the center and the periphery that characterizes space
in his novels reflects a broader concern with boundaries, borders, and
liminal spaces in Modiano's work. As Bruno Blanckeman has argued
convincingly, Modiano's Paris is defined by the narrator's relationship to the eighteenth arrondissement, a space that lies both inside
and above a city that itself lies both inside and above a certain traditional image of French identity: "a city, Paris, is grasped in turn from
this lone neighborhood as if it were both organic and external to it."[3]
Geographically central, Paris represents the beating heart of France,
the traditional locus of power for political, commercial, intellectual,
and artistic activities, the magnet that draws talent relentlessly from
the provinces. By contrast, however, Paris also serves as a site of encounter, an international, cosmopolitan, anonymous, and even neutral space that contrasts with the local flavor of the provinces. The
image of Paris that results from this juxtaposition is, to say the least,
contradictory: at once superlatively French and strikingly other, the
city mirrors the tensions inherent to the search for identity common
to all of Modiano's narrators.

These tensions extend to Modiano's use of real spaces in his
literary works. The generic instability of the novels—our faltering
sense of where we might situate them on a spectrum ranging from
fiction to autobiography—asks us to interrogate the status of places
as well as the characters that inhabit them. As Gellings explains,

2. Paul Gellings, "Le Nice de Modiano: Cartographie du royaume des ombres,"
La nouvelle revue française 589 (April 2009): 188. All translations are my own unless
otherwise indicated.
3. Bruno Blanckeman, "Droit de cité: Un Paris de Patrick Modiano," in *Lectures
de Modiano*, ed. Roger-Yves Roche (Nantes: Éditions Cécile Defaut, 2009), 172.

"It is easy to understand why such a narrative space is necessary, since, in a universe peopled with vain simulacra, we need reliable reference points to orient ourselves (with the possible result, certainly, of becoming buried in them)."[4] The resulting written places are both real and imaginary; for Alice Kaplan, "He's invented such a specific a notion of place that you can think of certain places as being 'Modianesque.'"[5] Modiano himself draws our attention to the uncertain status of literary space in *Dora Bruder* when he layers his wanderings through the Picpus neighborhood over Victor Hugo's description of Jean Valjean and Cosette's escape through the same area in *Les Misérables*. The resulting landscape bears a dreamlike quality:

> And suddenly, you have a sensation of vertigo, as if Cosette and Jean Valjean . . . have taken a leap into space: thus far, they have been following real Paris streets, and now, abruptly, Victor Hugo thrusts them into the imaginary district of Paris that he calls the Petit Picpus. It is the same sense of strangeness that overcomes you when you find yourself walking through an unfamiliar district in a dream. On waking, you realize, little by little, that the pattern of its streets had overlaid the one with which, in daytime, you are familiar.[6]

However, the unsettling nature of the dream does not merely consist in its topographically tentative relationship to reality; it is uncanny to the extent that, even fictionalized, even reimagined, this topography continues to intrude on the consciousness of the dreamer, the writer, or the reader, in order to *signify*. In this case, Cosette and Jean Valjean enter a fictional convent that Modiano identifies as Dora Bruder's very real refuge during the Occupation.

I propose to investigate the ways in which Modiano's topography signifies through the example of a city that is both peripheral and emotionally central to his work: Bordeaux, the bourgeois *belle endormie*, mythic agent of a social and cultural heritage that simultaneously attracts, eludes, and repulses its narrator. I will trace the possible meanings associated with Modiano's depiction of Bordeaux in three

4. Gellings, "Le Nice de Modiano," 188.

5. Kristi McGuire, "Alice Kaplan on Patrick Modiano," *The Chicago Blog*, University of Chicago Press, January 7, 2015, http://pressblog.uchicago.edu/2015/01/07/alice-kaplan-on-patrick-modiano.html.

6. Modiano, *Dora Bruder*, trans. Joanna Kilmartin (Berkeley: University of California Press, 1999), 41.

emblematic instances: Raphaël Schlemilovitch's search for roots in *La place de l'étoile*, Serge Alexandre's family reunion in *Ring Roads*, and Patrick Modiano's escape from boarding school in *Pedigree*. The juxtaposition of these three texts allows us to draw some preliminary conclusions about the use of Bordeaux as a signifying space in Modiano's work.[7] There is a temporal progression, from Modiano's first novel (1968), to his third and last in the Occupation Trilogy (1972), and to his turn toward literary nonfiction (2005) mirrored by his shift from fiction to autobiography. Each of these literary works is also, to a varying but noteworthy degree, focused on the figure of the father, the collaborationist Jew, a problematic and compelling character who is closely associated with Modiano's deployment of Bordeaux. Finally, the relative role of Bordeaux, at least in terms of the number of words and pages that trace its contours, decreases over time to the point that Modiano intimates, in *Pedigree*, that he hardly knows Bordeaux at all.

Much like Paris within France and Montmartre within Paris, *La place de l'étoile* constitutes both an outlier and an exemplum of Modiano's literary work; its layers of self-conscious pastiche and parody contain the hard kernel of elements that would define the later novels. Modiano has described *La place de l'étoile* as an attempt to engage with the discourses that helped shape his father's identity as a French Jew. The protagonist, Raphaël Schlemilovitch, is a man in search of an identity, a cosmopolitan in search of roots, and a narrator in search of a voice. For all of these reasons, his selection of Bordeaux as the site of his education is anything but arbitrary. Indeed, he immediately cites the literary and cultural weight that the city represents to justify his choice to his father: "Basically, I've decided to give up this shallow, decadent cosmopolitan life. I'm retiring to the provinces, the French countryside, back to the land [*le terroir*]. I've just settled on Bordeaux, the Guyenne, as a rest cure for my nerves. It's also a little homage to an old friend, François Mauriac."[8] The word *terroir* is important here; its specificity to French culture is highlighted by its multipart translation as "the French countryside . . . the land."

7. For a cinematic treatment of Bordeaux that incorporates many of the motifs found in Modiano's novels, see the 2003 film *Bon voyage*, directed by Jean-Paul Rappeneau and co-written by Rappeneau and Modiano.

8. Modiano, *La place de l'étoile*, trans. Frank Wynne, in *The Occupation Trilogy* (New York: Bloomsbury, 2015), 30. Hereafter cited in the text as *PE*.

Terroir implies not only a soil with its own microclimate that encourages the growth of specific plants, but also the connection between the product of the soil and the land that grew it. According to Schlemilovitch, "Paris was too much like me. An artificial flower in the middle of France. I was counting on Bordeaux to teach me true values, to put me in touch with the land [*le terroir*]" (*PE* 34–35). In short, by choosing Bordeaux and the *terroir* it represents, Schlemilovitch is choosing to transplant himself into a specific medium for growth. As he contemplates growing into this new identity, he also gestures toward a literary tradition that is rooted in the idea of *terroir*. François Mauriac, one of the "three Ms" of Bordeaux (Mauriac, Montesquieu, Montaigne), employs a Catholic, bourgeois, provincial aesthetic in his writing that embodies the traditional values of the city that produced him even as he critiques their weaknesses.

Schlemilovitch's journey to Bordeaux represents more than an opportunity to re-root himself in new soil; it allows him to imagine a new past and a new future that insert him in an honorable lineage and trajectory. This simultaneous historical and geographical positioning emphasizes the palimpsestic nature of space and time in Modiano's novels and encourages us to view Bordeaux as a place in which the sediments of past and future are always available in the present. Akane Kawakami emphasizes this key aspect of Modiano's "textual geographies": "Such geographical locations function in the same way as the palimpsest, that well-worn spatial metaphor for time, popular because of the impression it gives of tangible layers of the past."[9] As Schlemilovitch gazes through the transparent yet real limit of the train window—his access to *la France profonde* both immediate and constrained—he reinvents a lineage that extends into both past and future. "I was no longer called Raphaël Schlemilovitch," he imagines. "I was the eldest son of a notary from Libourne and we were heading back to our home in the country" (*PE* 32). His re-implantation and re-growth in the *terroir* recasts his eventual return to Paris as an honorable, even glorious step in a bourgeois trajectory: "In June I would pass the entrance exam to the *École Normale Supérieure*. I would definitively 'go up' to Paris. On the Rue d'Ulm, I would share rooms with a young provincial lad like myself . . . We would be part of our

9. Akane Kawakami, *A Self-Conscious Art: Patrick Modiano's Postmodern Fictions* (Liverpool: Liverpool University Press, 2000), 59. See esp. the section on "textual geographies," 56–60.

country's elite. Our brains would be in Paris but our hearts would
ever remain in the provinces" (*PE* 31–32). The use of the *futur simple*
in the original French text underlines the nature of these projected
events, both distant and certain. We can contrast them to the narrator's closing words to his father, after arriving in Bordeaux: "I'm going
to die before very long. I've just got time to pass the entrance exam to
the *École Normale Supérieure*, the first stage of assimilation. I promise you your grandson will be a Maréchal de France. Oh yes, I am
planning to try and reproduce" (*PE* 38–39). Here we can already see
the hesitation that enters into the narrator's plans; in the near future,
the *futur proche*, he anticipates two actions: trying and dying, and
projects glory onto a future that no longer includes him. The fraught
phase of "assimilation" is invoked without elaboration; the passage
from rootless transplant to product of a *terroir* is occluded in favor of
the passage from production to reproduction.

   What has occurred between the narrator's arrival in Bordeaux and
his father's departure to alter his tranquil re-imagination of his past
and confident plans for his own future? The narrator presents us with
a schematic overview of the cityscape, briefly evoking a handful of
landmarks: the Gare Saint-Jean, the Rue Sainte-Catherine, Tourny.[10]
But the overwhelming sensation evoked by this section of the Bordeaux interlude is one of déjà vu: a confusing array of streets, people,
and events are layered on top of other streets, people, and events that
seem to belie Schlemilovitch's later assertion that "Paris is not Bordeaux" (*PE* 46). From the moment they leave the train station in a
taxi, the narrator and his father play a "game" in which they confound past and present, Paris and Bordeaux to create a narrative of
intrigue and danger. The narrator initiates this game by assimilating
their taxi driver to the Gestapo and the streets of Bordeaux to the
Rue Lauriston in Paris, where the headquarters of the French Gestapo
were located. Their hotel, the Splendid, is indistinguishable from the
international luxury hotels[11] that the narrator and his father have fre-

10. Each of these sites is associated in some way with World War II or the Jewish
experience in Bordeaux. The Gare Saint-Jean was the site from which rail convoys departed for Drancy during World War II. The Rue Sainte-Catherine was the primary site
of "Jewish heritage, business, and housing" until the neighborhood was pillaged during
the Occupation (Gérard Nahon, *Juifs et judaïsme à Bordeaux* [Bordeaux: Mollat, 2003],
306). I will return to Tourny later in the article.
   11. See Modiano, *La place de l'étoile*, 34. Wynne translates "palaces internatio-
naux" as "grand hotels."

quented in Paris. Yet in spite of its generic attributes, including its foreign-sounding name that attests to a "naïve anglophilia,"[12] this hotel has a history that the narrator chooses not to reveal: its halls witnessed encounters among members of the dying Third Republic, the new collaborationist regime, the occupying force, and Bordeaux society.[13] This non-place is, in fact, a *place* that only appears anonymous and interchangeable.[14] The allusion to this occluded history is underscored when Schlemilovitch and his father are targeted by a disquieting "operation rat extermination" (*PE* 38) that echoes the roundups and deportations of foreign, then French Jews that began in July 1942 in Bordeaux and continued throughout the Occupation.[15] Indeed, in the words of Sylvie Guillaume and Bernard Lachaise, "historiography presents Bordeaux as one of the most collaborationist cities in France."[16] In other words, the promise of the *terroir*, the literary and cultural image of Bordeaux that the narrator has formed, remains elusive as a direct result of the historical events that are present, yet effaced, within the city's public and semi-public spaces.

Schlemilovitch is persuaded to leave Bordeaux following a chance meeting with Charles Lévy-Vendôme, a paternal figure who invites him to take part in the white slave trade. By fulfilling the "orders" of wealthy foreigners, Schlemilovitch will ensure that the national body of France is desecrated through the spoliation of its provincial virgins. This revenge is framed as a historical consequence of the marginalization of the other and can most readily be associated with the impact of World War II on the narrator's identity as a French Jew.

12. Isabelle Dangy, "Hôtels, cafés, et villas tristes: Lieux privés et lieux publics dans les romans de Modiano," in *Lectures de Modiano*, ed. Roger-Yves Roche (Nantes: Éditions Cécile Defaut, 2009), 186.

13. For example, Dominique Lormier cites an event, hosted by the occupant and attended by members of high society, that took place at the Splendid-Hotel in 1940. See Lormier, *Bordeaux brûle-t-il? La libération de la Gironde 1940–1945* (Bordeaux: Les Dossiers d'Aquitaine, 1998), 43.

14. I rely here on the distinction that Marc Augé makes between places and non-places: "If a place can be defined as relational, historical and concerned with identity, then a space which cannot be defined as relational, or historical, or concerned with identity will be a non-place." Augé, *Non-Places: Introduction to an Anthropology of Supermodernity*, trans. John Howe (London: Verso, 1992), 77–78.

15. For a summary of the Jewish experience in Bordeaux under the Occupation, see Nahon, "Statuts des juifs, spoliation, déportation, liquidation 1940–1944," in *Juifs et judaïsme à Bordeaux*, 285–318.

16. Sylvie Guillaume and Bernard Lachaise, "Le politique," in *Histoire des Bordelais*, ed. Pierre Guillaume (Bordeaux: Mollat, 2002), 220.

However, the description of a specific buyer implies something much broader: "an emir who wants to avenge himself for Charles Martel," the Beirut-based client is seeking an "elegant French girl whose ancestors fought in the crusades. Good provincial landed gentry" (*PE* 49–50). The drive for revenge is thus attributed here to a Muslim who is aided and abetted by two Jews, and the reference to Beirut implicates the wider francophone world. In this short exchange, then, we find a critique of French domination that has been articulated in various forms throughout Modiano's body of work.

The Algerian War and World War II are frequently juxtaposed in Modiano's novels when the narrator's historical context (1960s) reminds him of his father's experiences (1940s). These two time periods are interpenetrable; their boundaries are fluid. While incomparable in many respects, they evoke a similar feeling of marginalization and danger for the narrator. From this crucible emerges the complex, contradictory archetype of the collaborationist Jew. The white slave trade serves as a kind of recasting of that collaboration; Schlemilovitch is an enemy of the state because he literally perverts the embodiments of its purity, and Lévy-Vendôme is a traitor because he perverts its language by attributing his own erotic writings to the luminaries of classical French literature. These perversions have, as their historical underpinning, Bordeaux's particular role as one of the eighteenth-century slave-trading capitals of France.[17] The "golden age" of Bordeaux, with its resulting elegant bourgeois façades lining the left bank of the Garonne, was built on the back of colonial trade, including the provisioning and launching of ships that visited the West Coast of Africa and the Antilles on their triangular route. Much like the misleading façades of the sixteenth *arrondissement* in Paris that Modiano describes elsewhere, the façades of Bordeaux belie the historic conditions that shaped them. They are part of a mythic imaginary that extends to the inhabitants of the city itself: "Behind this façade [on the waterfront], the central continuities are inscribed. From the Grand-Théâtre to Gambetta and Tourny by way of the Triangle with its refined businesses, they complete the inscription of Bordeaux's urban practices within the self-assured and prideful framework of a golden age of power and tradition."[18] Lévy-Vendôme's pointed refer-

17. See Éric Saugéra, *Bordeaux, port négrier, XVIIe–XIXe siècles* (Paris: Éditions Karthala, 2002) for a history of Bordeaux's implication in the slave trade.
18. Jean Dumas, "Le cadre urbain des Bordelais," in *Histoire des Bordelais*, 13.

ence to the French Gestapo ("I met them at Bonny and Laffont's place on Rue Lauriston," *PE* 51) supports the comparison.

Modiano's second integration of Bordeaux into his narrator's biography can be found in *Ring Roads*, the last novel in the Occupation Trilogy. Addressing his father, Modiano's narrator, Serge Alexandre, claims to turn the page: "I tell you again that I'll stay with you until the end of this book, the last one dealing with my other life."[19] Thus the narrator gives the novel to us as a product of his own imagination and research, his own writing. The effect, doubled by the use of an avowedly false name, is to confound the narrator and the author, nudging the novel into a zone of uncertainty between fiction and nonfiction. And because this is, openly and explicitly, a book about the narrator's father and his tenuous relationship with his son, the return to Bordeaux is again predicated on developments in their relationship. In contrast to Schlemilovitch's measured decision to adopt Bordeaux as the *terroir* in which to reform his identity, Serge Alexandre finds himself there as the direct result of his father's abandonment. Left in the care of an elderly woman, confined to a boarding school, attached to a disdainful bourgeois family, the narrator spends his formative years in the environs of Bordeaux while nonetheless remaining alien to its cultural norms. It is almost as though Schlemilovitch's dream of reinventing a past and a family have been realized, yet have resulted in a similar failure to assimilate. Serge Alexandre describes a childhood home in Libourne, a secondary education in Bordeaux, and access to the home and family life of the wine aristocracy of Bordeaux. His spatial grasp of Bordeaux is broader and more socially respectable: the Pessac family, whose very name corresponds to a suburban area of Bordeaux that became known as a health resort for the city's bourgeoisie,[20] as well as a wine-producing area, lives in the dockside neighborhood of Chartrons, known for its close association with the wine trade. Even so, he once again ends up in the Hôtel Splendid with his outrageously dressed, socially awkward father, in whose company he commonly finds himself identified as a criminal. "You were sneaking away like a thief?" Monsieur Pessac asks pointedly, causing the narrator to reflect that this "sentence is burned into my memory, because it was true that we looked just like a couple of

19. Modiano, *Ring Roads*, trans. Caroline Hillier and Frank Wynne, in *The Occupation Trilogy* (New York: Bloomsbury, 2015), 303.
20. Dumas, "Le cadre urbain des Bordelais," 15.

thieves caught red-handed . . . leaving me feeling as though we had broken into this bourgeois mansion."[21] And indeed, the act that leads to this conflation of the narrator and his father with thieves is the former's attempt to recover a box of books that he had hidden in the family's closet. By reclaiming these novels, and thus the literature they represent, Serge Alexandre is in fact stealing something precious from these stereotypical representatives of social order in Bordeaux, an act that echoes Lévy-Vendôme's literary perversions.

Bordeaux is deployed as a nonfictional backdrop to the autobiographical events in its narrator's life in *Pedigree;* the first-person narrator of this text is assumed to correspond more or less exactly to Modiano. Here we find the shortest passage about the city, which is conversely filled with the most precise listing of landmarks. As Jean Dumas comments:

> In a framework as solidly structured as [Bordeaux], the age of the buildings gives an almost immutable status to everything that corresponds to the city's habits; permanence imposes itself in spite of modifications. The central and monumental Bordeaux . . . of the Belle Époque is, in its designations, the same as the city of the 1950s and, at least in its essential components, much the same today.[22]

The Allées de Tourny conjure up an enduring, almost mythical vision of Bordeaux as well as a phantasmal allusion to their namesake, the eighteenth-century French administrator whose legacy includes the beautification of the city at the height of its glory as well as an attempt to regulate the status of Jews living in Bordeaux. To the attuned reader, his name simultaneously contains the germ of Bordeaux as an elegant, bourgeois cityscape and the precarious status of one of the oldest and most established Jewish communities in France.

As in *La place de l'étoile,* the narrator attempts to flee his father; this time, instead of running through Tourny as a "joke," this iteration of the narrator takes off in front of the Grand Théâtre.[23] The Grand Théâtre is a symbolically fraught place to undertake such an escape, if we choose to read it as a literary signifier rather than a simple geographical landmark. It brings the issue of entwined French and Jewish identities to the forefront and grounds them in the his-

21. Modiano, *Ring Roads,* 260.
22. Dumas, "Le cadre urbain des Bordelais," 9.
23. See Modiano, *Pedigree: A Memoir,* trans. Mark Polizzotti (New Haven, CT: Yale University Press, 2015), 104.

torical context of World War II. In June 1940, the French government
fled Paris in the hopes of maintaining the Third Republic on French
soil, or, barring that, of establishing a new government in exile. They
first stopped in Tours before continuing south to Bordeaux, ahead of
the advancing German army. The Grand Théâtre serves as a kind of
shorthand for the Third Republic here: Bordeaux was the seat of government in 1870 when France was faced with a crushing German
defeat and the parliament held its sessions at the theater. The entire
history of the Third Republic is thus bookended between two crises
involving Germany that played out politically, at least in part, in central Bordeaux. The Third Republic was born in Bordeaux and it died
there in June 1940. We find a pointed allusion to this period in *La
place de l'étoile*:

> Ah, Raphaël, how I wish you had been in Bordeaux in June 1940! Picture
> the outrageous scenes! Gentlemen with beards and black frockcoats!
> University students! Ministers of the RÉ-PU-BLI-QUE are chattering
> away! Making grand gestures! Réda Caire and Maurice Chevalier are
> singing songs! Suddenly—BANG!—blond bare-chested youths burst
> into the Café du Commerce! They start a wholesale massacre! The
> gentlemen in frockcoats are thrown against the ceiling. They slam
> into the walls, crash into the rows of bottles. They splash about in
> puddles of Pernod, heads slashed by broken glass! The manageress,
> a woman named Marianne, is running this way and that. She gives
> little cries. The woman's an old whore! THE SLUT! [LA GUEUSE] Her
> skirt falls off. She's gunned down in a hail of machine gunfire (*PE* 44).

The Grand Café du Commerce et de Tourny was an elegant site for
meetings of the influential, housed in a nineteenth-century building
on the Allées de Tourny, within sight of the Grand Théâtre that had
once served as the seat of Republican power. Marianne, of course, is a
symbol of the French Republic and its principles of freedom and resistance. Her bust adorns the *mairies* of France and her profile graces the
official logo of the French Republic. *La Gueuse*, or The Slut, meanwhile, is the traditional epithet associated with the Third Republic by
its detractors; the Republic's personification in female form is figured
here in the person of the Café du Commerce's manageress, whose
slaughter mirrors the collapse of the Third Republic in both geographical proximity and gendered imagery. In *Pedigree*, the narrator's flight
away from his father, and ultimately back to Paris, can therefore be
read as a kind of reversal of the government's abandonment of the

capital. Could it not then represent a will to resistance that exceeds simple defiance of a father's orders?

Reading Modiano's work chronologically through the geographical lens of Bordeaux allows us to better grasp some of the defining characteristics of his writing as well as the enduring questions about historical memory and spaces of belonging that he raises. The progression from a writing style characterized by its excess and abundant use of pastiche to the increasingly spare *"petite musique"* of the later novels is mirrored by a nominally descriptive use of geographical space that ultimately gives way to an almost purely indexical use. Schlemilovitch evokes "this city of distinguished tradition, in this illustrious night that smelled of vintage wine and English tobacco" (*PE* 37). Bordeaux is a city that conjures up objects, natives "weighted down with cheeses and Saint-Émilion" (*PE* 33), one in which characters enter and interact, however superficially, with the spaces they name (a hotel, a nightclub, a school office, a dormitory, a classroom, a café). These spaces are largely generic, easily confounded with others of the same type and therefore, in a certain respect, indicative of a stereotypical depiction of Bordeaux. The city is framed as both too meaningful and too empty, a kind of void filled only with the weight of its representations, "a parallel universe, built on diverse connotations."[24] In other words, *La place de l'étoile* pastiches representations of the city as an avatar of French identity just as it pastiches discourses surrounding Jewishness. Its logic relies more on stereotype than history. This is less true in *Ring Roads*, which transmits specific values in correlation to geographical space through the mediation of books and heirlooms, and not true in *Pedigree*, where place names are vested with meaning by the reader or not at all. In her analysis of the "effet d'irréel" in Modiano's novels, Kawakami argues that although proper names such as those denoting places do not need to be recognized by the reader to maintain the legibility of the text, they are nonetheless invested with the possibility of a "moral impact" on the enlightened reader.[25]

Modiano's Bordeaux, then, is a city constructed out of multiple maps: topographical, historical, cultural, and literary. It is a collaborative construction, too, one that implicates the reader in the creation of a space that is not only legible but also meaningful. Michael

24. Gellings, "Le Nice de Modiano," 196.
25. Kawakami, *A Self-Conscious Art*, 82–83.

Rothberg's concept of "multidirectional memory" constitutes a useful framework through which to read the sites of memory and forgetting that mark Modiano's map of Bordeaux: "subject to ongoing negotiation, cross-referencing, and borrowing . . . productive and not privative."[26] The intersectional nature of memory in Modiano's work, the imbrication of different layers of history, lends itself particularly well to a geographical analysis that maps the intersections of memory onto the intersections of streets. As the narrator of *The Night Watch* laments, "You try to forget the past, but your footsteps invariably lead you back to difficult crossroads [*intersections*]."[27] Like Raphaël Schlemilovitch, we can read the city as a text—or the text as a city—that allows us to imagine alternative pasts and futures; but those pasts and futures are always already constrained by a history, whether or not we recognize its signposts. Like other key sites in the Modianosphere—the Right Bank of Paris and the Promenade des Anglais in Nice, for example—Bordeaux has continued to acquire new sediments of meaning since it served as a setting for Modiano's narrators. Bordeaux, with its collaborationist reputation, is also the city in which collaborationist policies were formally condemned through the 1998 conviction of Maurice Papon. Like Modiano reading Dora into *Les Misérables*, our continued reading of Modiano's Bordeaux through a contemporary lens—one that takes into account the past, present, and future—is entirely in line with the shifting terrain he has charted for us.

26. Michael Rothberg, "Introduction: Theorizing Multidirectional Memory in a Transnational Age," in *Multidirectional Memory: Remembering the Holocaust in the Age of Decolonization* (Stanford: Stanford University Press, 2009), 3.

27. Modiano, *The Night Watch*, trans. Patricia Wolf and Frank Wynne, in *The Occupation Trilogy* (New York: Bloomsbury, 2015), 183.

RICHARD J. GOLSAN

Modiano's Catharsis: *Dora Bruder*, *Un pedigree*, and Beyond[1]

MODIANO'S TRAGIC VISION

In an important 1986 essay, "Re-Membering Modiano, or Something Happened," Gerald Prince offers a concise and—in light of Modiano's subsequent body of work—prescient summation of the novelist's aims, accomplishments, and vision as a writer. Prince emphasizes the continuity of Modiano's novels in thematic and structural terms, noting his use of "classic themes" including "the self, the quest, love and death, Oedipus and Theseus, Abraham and Isaac, time memory."[2] He also underscores crucial paradoxes at the heart of Modiano's *oeuvre*. The first paradox concerns the apparent contradiction between the limpidity of the writer's prose and the lack of closure in virtually all of Modiano's early works. The "indisputable readability" of his classically French *récits*, the grace, sobriety, precision, and purity of his style (42)—and the implicit promise of resolution—are ultimately undermined by the fact that, as Prince writes,

> [t]he story-line repeatedly dissolves: narrative modes of organization are not adequate to the discontinuity of the past, memory, life (. . .) and the narration—elliptical, hesitant, wandering—breaks into bits and pieces (. . .) and presents quite a story without telling one. The self is not illuminated. The quest comes to no end . . . The riddle cannot be solved. (43)

The second paradox concerns Modiano's and his characters' inability to come to terms with the weight of the past in any defini-

---

1. This essay is for Nancy.
2. Gerald Prince, "Re-Membering Modiano, or Something Happened," *SubStance* 15/1 (1986): 42.

YFS 133, *"Detecting" Patrick Modiano*, ed. Golsan and Higgins, © 2018 by Yale University.

tive or fulfilling sense. For the novelist, "to be free of the past people should have no memory and should not even suspect that they have one (39)." But, at the same time in Modiano's fictional world, "the past cannot be left alone" (39). Indeed, his characters are all too often condemned to a kind of endless and Sisyphean struggle with it. The discovery of what Modiano labels in *Vestiaire d'enfance* a "Switzerland of the heart" where the narrator finds happiness in no longer having a memory, where "amnesia thicken[s] everyday like a hardening skin," and where there is no longer past or future, turns out in most instances in Modiano's fiction to be short-lived, if not entirely illusory.[3]

The reason for this inability to escape the past, in Modiano's case, has precisely to do with which past is being referred to. The past in question is, as Prince defines it, "The Occupation. Drancy. Auschwitz" (37). There, "Something happened," something irremediable. As Modiano states in his Nobel Lecture, for him the Occupation and, more specifically, the Paris of the Dark Years mark his "night of origins," his "original night" without which he would never have been born.[4] He is himself the product of one of the many romantic chance encounters that would never have happened in peacetime. All throughout his work, the Occupation is also *un passé qui ne passe pas* (a past that does not pass).[5] Modiano claims to have real memories from that time, memories from before his birth in 1945. In *Dora Bruder* he laments the disappearance that same year of "so many friends" who died fighting in the Resistance or were swept away in the Holocaust. In this sense, the Dark Years are also a source of profound and tragic loss from which the writer, as well as many of his characters, can never recover. In effect, novelist and characters are essentially survivors of that traumatic event. They must therefore experience, even at a distance or obliquely, the anger, shame,

3. The link between amnesia, or lack of memory, and freedom or salvation is a common theme in Modiano's work, as is the metaphor a "Switzerland of the heart" or a "Swiss village." At the conclusion of *Livret de famille* (Paris: Gallimard, 1977), Modiano describes his daughter sleeping peacefully on his shoulder, with nothing troubling her sleep, because "She did not yet have a memory" (215). In *Dora Bruder*, Modiano describes the destruction of the old houses on the Rue des Jardins-Saint-Paul and their replacement with modern, anonymous row houses as the construction of a sort of "Swiss village."

4. Patrick Modiano, "Discours à l'Académie suédoise" (Paris: Gallimard, 2015).

5. I am borrowing here the title of Eric Conan and Henry Rousso's 1995 book, *Vichy. Un passé qui ne passe pas.*

impotence and, later, the numbness and detachment from the present that so many survivor narratives underscore. Where feelings of shame and impotence are concerned, Primo Levy, in his essay "The Truce," stresses the reactions of Russian soldiers upon discovering Levy's *lager* "packed with corpses and dying prisoners":

> It was the same shame which we knew so well, which submerged us after the selections, and every time we had to witness or undergo an outrage; the shame that the Germans never knew, the shame which the just man experiences when confronted by a crime committed by another, and he feels remorse because of its existence, because of it having been irrevocably introduced into the world of existing things, and because his will has proven nonexistent or feeble and was incapable of putting up a good defense. (72)[6]

Modiano's "survivors"—including the novelist himself—are for the most part not among those who witness firsthand the shock and horror of the Holocaust. They do not, to paraphrase Prince's title, experience the "Something" that "happened" directly. Rather, they are those who to all appearances experience a sort of numbness or detachment by way of an "aftershock," or who seem prone to interpose more innocuous Freudian "screen memories" between themselves and the real source of their trauma. They fixate on "missing persons" and forgotten places or, like the writer himself, are endlessly fascinated by names in phone books, street addresses that have disappeared, and so on. This fixation and detachment might also explain a characteristic of many of Modiano's first-person narrators, and of the narration itself. According to Akane Kawakami, Modiano's narrator is reticence personified, never revealing much of himself, and rarely demonstrating or articulating any emotional response whatsoever. More importantly, perhaps, there is also "a strange emptiness to him . . . a comparative lack of character."[7] He is "discreetly identity-less, occupying the space of the world while not filling it" (10). He does not "impose a psychological hue on the narrative" and, as Franck Salaun stresses, the situations he de-

6. The passage in question is quoted in the essay "Shame" in Primo Levy, *The Drowned and the Saved*, trans. Raymond Rosenthal (New York: Simon and Schuster, 1988).

7. Akane Kawakami, *A Self-Conscious Art: Patrick Modiano's Postmodern Fictions* (Liverpool: Liverpool University Press, 2000), 9.

scribes are generally "devoid of moral judgements, of good and bad conscience." He leaves "vacant the place of sentiment and of value judgements."[8] In the end, Modiano's narrators generally furnish only an "impersonal and pre-individual archaeology," of places, people, and situations.

To the degree that Modiano's narrators—and the novels themselves—are largely devoid of psychological "hues" or interpretations imposed by novelist and/or narrator, and to the extent that the characters' fates often seem determined by large and ominous events over whose memories, traces, and impact they have no control —"magnetic fields," as Modiano refers to them in *Dora Bruder*[9]—they bear comparison to the tragedies of antiquity. Like the tragic heroes of Aeshylus and Sophocles, the destinies of Modiano's protagonists are all too often shaped by crimes and their consequences that occurred in the past, even before their births, crimes that at best they only vaguely glimpse but that they seek nevertheless to discover and resolve. But while Oedipus must—and does—discover that he murdered his own father, and then, knowing the truth, experiences a form of catharsis in accepting his fate, and while Orestes must avenge the murder of his father by murdering his mother and her lover to experience the same effect, such cathartic moments, such moments of recognition and clarity, are rare in Modiano's work. As Prince stresses, in Modiano's work story lines evaporate, quests do not achieve their goal, and riddles and mysteries remain unsolved. Moreover, the limpidity of Modiano's prose, so geared to the task of revelation, ultimately fails in this task. In this sense, Modiano's tragic vision appears to be a quintessentially modern one, reminiscent, for example, of Beckett's in *Waiting for Godot*. For Modiano and for many of his protagonists, to quote Serge Doubrovsky, "Human drama becomes tragedy when there is no more *dénouement* or meaning at the end, when suffering brings no ultimate redemption, and misfortune no longer possesses the certitude of triumphant tomorrows."[10] In the end, no existential balance is—or can be—redressed, no *Dike* vanquishing *Adikia*, no justice vanquishing injustice. Catharsis—both as "the ultimate

8. Franck Salaun, cited in *Ibid.*, 12.
9. Modiano, *Dora Bruder*, trans. Joanna Kilmartin (Berkeley: University of California Press, 1999), 209. All references to *Dora Bruder* are to this edition.
10. Quoted in Jean-Marie Domenach, *Le retour du tragique* (Paris: Seuil, 1967), 276.

illumination which shall turn a painful story into a profound and moving experience,"[11] and as "the elimination of a complex by bringing it to consciousness and affording it expression"[12]—seems all but impossible in Modiano's fictional universe.

MODIANO'S CATHARSIS

Or is it? Modiano's tragic vision appears to be fundamentally a static one, one that reiterates itself in one form or another from work to work. This impression is reinforced by the repetition of stock characters and themes. For example, Leo Robson characterizes Modiano's "Super-novel, or "novel cut-out" as a "male narrator estranged from his parents, in love with an ethereal girl who disappeared, and liable to transcribe phone numbers and unfamiliar pan-European names." The Modianesque narrator also "mourns an adored, long-dead brother" and compulsively visits and revisits the Rue Lauriston, home to the French Gestapo during the Occupation.[13] While obviously reductive, Robson's assessment of Modiano's "novel cut-out" does underscore a repetitiveness that the novelist clearly embraces.

In his Nobel Lecture, Modiano offers two possible explanations for such fictional repetitions. First, "each new book, at the moment of its writing erases the preceding one to the point that I have the impression of having forgotten it" (12). Second, and perhaps more crucially, Modiano affirms that, despite his fascination with the historical moment of the Occupation, like other writers he "also always expresses . . . something atemporal [eternal?]" (18) in his works. In this light, the stock characters and themes comprise crucial components of his personal mythology. And, as in Greek Tragedy from Aeschylus to Euripides, the novelist draws repeatedly on these mythological ingredients to build his own "tragedies."

Modiano's remarks point to a fundamental immutability in his "tragic vision" and imply not only an absence of catharsis in his writing but also, as a consequence, a lack of evolution or progression in his oeuvre as a whole. Two texts, however, call these assumptions

11. H.D.F. Kitto, *Greek Tragedy*, (Garden City, NY: Doubleday-Anchor Books, 1954), 147.

12. *Webster's Ninth Collegiate Dictionary* (Springfield, MA: Merriam-Webster, 1987), 216.

13. Leo Robson, "Why nobody knows what to think about Patrick Modiano," *New Statesman*, 13 October 2014.

into question: *Dora Bruder* and Modiano's memoir, *Un pedigree*.[14] *Dora Bruder* recounts the novelist's fascination with and investigation of the fate of a (real-life) victim of the Holocaust, Dora Bruder, deported with her father in September 1942 to Auschwitz. *Un pedigree* offers a moving and often disturbing account of Modiano's early years, and especially his painful and occasionally tortured relationship with his parents. So close are the two works in tone and theme, so intimately interconnected are they that one has the impression they were written back to back. In fact, *Dora Bruder* and *Un pedigree* were written—or published at least—eight years apart, in 1997 and 2005 respectively. Three novels, *Des inconnus*, *La petite bijou*, and *Accident nocturne* were published in the intervening period.

I will argue here first that, even though separated by almost a decade, *Dora Bruder* and *Un pedigree* represent two stages of a single catharsis, and that the second stage is not possible without the first. Moreover, the catharsis that spans across the two works addresses the two fundamental sources of trauma in Modiano's life and work: his very troubled relationship with his parents—his father in particular—and the terrible crisis and sense of loss the Occupation, or more precisely the memory of it, represents for him.

Although much of Modiano's work deals with the Dark Years of World War II, starting with what is now generally referred to in English as the "Occupation Trilogy," *Dora Bruder* is the first and only work that focuses intensely and relentlessly on the Holocaust and French complicity in it, often in concise documentary terms. Modiano tells the story of Dora Bruder and her family, as well as that of other individuals who ultimately became the victims of Hitler's Final Solution. These victims include a certain Robert Tartakovsky, arrested and deported in June 1942, whose deeply affecting letter to his mother following his arrest, discovered by chance by the writer in a book stall along the Seine, is quoted in full. They also include Annette Zelman, a young Jewish girl in love with Jean Jausion. After meeting in Paris, the two fled to the Unoccupied Zone to protect her. Jausion's parents, we learn, denounced her to the Germans to prevent the couple from marrying, apparently not realizing that she

14. All citations here are from Mark Polizzotti's English translation *Pedigree, a Memoir*. (New Haven: Yale UP, 2015). I am using the original French title here because, as Lynn Higgins rightly observes, it underscores the "sadness" and "anonymity" of the writer's lineage. (Conversation with the author.)

would not be returned to her family as they had requested, but rather deported. Later, the reader learns that Jausion *fils* died in an apparent suicide attack, ramming his car into and shooting at a column of German soldiers. Modiano also addresses the fate of Albert Schaky, a young Jew who had joined the Resistance, was arrested and deported, and died in Dachau in 1944. Known as le Zébu, Schaky, Modiano recounts, had earlier lived in the writer's bedroom on the Quai de Conti. Modiano also expresses sympathy for a Jewish girl forced into burglary in order to survive who was arrested in the act, deported, and died. The list goes on.

But Modiano's relentless pursuit of documentary evidence over several years,[15] as well as the tireless focus of his novelistic imagination, centers ultimately on the adolescent runaway Dora Bruder, her mother, and especially her father. The documentary evidence assembled includes a *petite annonce* in *Paris Soir* in 1941 that launches the writer's search; photographs of Dora and her family (in the English language edition); testimony (recounted second hand) from Dora's surviving relative, a cousin; and the parents' Jewish dossier (the material gathered at the Commisariat de police on Jews during the Occupation), as well as other archival documents. All of this information is enriched by Modiano's remarkable erudition concerning the Paris of the Dark Years.

What Modiano learns of Dora and her family is heartbreaking, even before their deaths at Auschwitz. Remembered for his "gentleness" and "kindness" by his niece and Dora's cousin, Ernst Bruder led a difficult life before arriving in Paris. A veteran of the Great War, he had signed up for the French Foreign Legion to escape post-war Vienna. He then endured the harsh conditions of fighting in the Legion in North Africa, where Modiano the novelist imagines him dreaming of home: "At night, in the landscape of stone-strewn sand, did he dream of Vienna, the city of his birth, and the chestnut trees of the Hauptallee?" (19). Wounded in battle, Bruder was declared one hundred percent disabled, and dismissed from the Legion. Subsequently he went to Paris where, despite his disability, he did manual labor, apparently under very harsh conditions. Modiano surmises that he was not even let off work to register his daughter's birth. A friend had to do that. Modiano underscores the tragic irony of the fact that the only official

---

15. For an account of the role played by Serge Klarsfeld in obtaining this evidence, and also the relations between the two men, see Maryline Heck's article in this volume.

mention he found of Bruder's disability "was in the police files designed to facilitate the roundups during the Occupation" (19).

Although described in less detail than Ernst Bruder, Dora's mother also led a difficult life. An immigrant from Budapest, Cecile Burdej lost three sisters to typhoid fever within a month of arriving in the French capital. She survived her husband and daughter during the Occupation, but only by a few months, before being deported herself. Summing up, Modiano writes of Ernst and Cecile Burdej: "They are the sort of people who leave few traces" (20).

But it is of course Dora whose fate and brief life fascinates, indeed obsesses the writer. He spent years tracking down even the most basic information about Dora: her birth date, her address, her parents' names and backgrounds, Dora's attendance at a Catholic school, and most importantly, her flights from the school and the four months she spent in hiding before being arrested and eventually deported. That Modiano feels viscerally connected to Dora and identifies with her,[16] is evident not only in his relentless pursuit of even the smallest details of her brief existence, but also in his expressed empathy for her, an empathy that exceeds that which the novelist usually displays toward his characters. He imagines her flight from school as he remembers his own adolescent fugue; he pictures her returning to school after her initial flight like it "was going back to prison" (37). Describing a late photo of her with her mother and grandmother, Modiano speaks of her "expression of sad sweetness and defiance" (75). So close does the writer feel to Dora and her family that he experiences "this sense of absence, of emptiness, whenever I find myself in places they had lived" (21). On several occasions in *Dora Bruder*, he has the impression of walking in her footsteps.

The writer's empathy for and identification with Dora achieve their most sustained expression and emotional power in his description of Dora's fate following her arrest and in the days and weeks before her deportation. Modiano documents the identities of other young women rounded up and also taken to Tourelles prison. He mentions four girls arrested with Dora, who are taken to Pithiviers

---

16. For an excellent discussion of Modiano's identification and empathy for with Dora Bruder, and the implications of that connection taken in a different direction from the one I am taking here, see Susan Rubin Suleiman, "Oneself as Other: Identification and Mourning in Patrick Modiano's *Dora Bruder*," *Studies in 20th- and 21st-Century Literature* 31/2 (2007): 32–50.

rather than being deported directly to Auschwitz. Although like them a French citizen, Dora apparently declines to leave with them. In his most dramatic—and revealing—act of identification with Dora, Modiano imagines her motives and writes that the reason she stayed behind was "easy to guess": she wished to remain with her father, whom she had recently found again after his own arrest. Father and daughter, Modiano writes, were deported together to their deaths at Auschwitz on 18 September 1942.

Dora Bruder constitutes Modiano's most relentless exploration, and indeed his most direct and explicit confrontation with the horrors of Paris in Dark Years and the nightmare of the Holocaust; there is no room in the work for the mysterious and vaguely ethereal characters in so much of his fiction. The individuals discussed in *Dora Bruder* are real, historical persons whose fates, individually and collectively, are deeply and profoundly tragic. Moreover, in the orchestration of their respective demises around, and leading up to Dora's deportation and death, they tend to *amplify* the tragedy of her own fate. In presenting them in this fashion, Modiano the narrator acts as a kind of tragic chorus. In the process, Dora Bruder becomes not just a name among the thousands, the millions, without human identity or substance, disappeared forever in the Holocaust, but an exemplary figure of that crime, a tragic heroine of sorts, who lives again through Modiano's writing.

But the cathartic moment that closes *Dora Bruder* belongs ultimately less to the adolescent girl than to the writer himself. In pursuing the traces of Dora Bruder over many years, as is so often *not* the case with many of his fictional heroes or stand-ins, Modiano discovers the truth and solves the riddle of her existence. He learns Dora's fate, and thereby brings closure to her life as well as to the lives of the other victims described in the work. But the truth, the wisdom is gleaned not simply by plumbing the depths and horror of the Holocaust, of experiencing as directly as possible through Dora the "something" irrevocable that has happened. Truth and wisdom are also found in moving beyond the horror, and experiencing a form of redemption or salvation through it. Discussing the fate of le Zébu near the end of *Dora Bruder*, Modiano recognizes and acknowledges that "he (le Zébu) and others like him had taken all the punishments meted out to them in order that we should suffer no more than pinpricks" (82). In the final lines of *Dora Bruder*, Modiano also understands that even Dora herself in one sense had ultimately escaped, perhaps even transcended, the crushing weight of her own tragic destiny by preserving the "secret" of her flight:

> I shall never know how she spent her days, where she hid, in whose company she passed the winter months of her first escape, or the few weeks of spring when she escaped for the second time. That is her secret. A poor and precious secret that not even the executioners, the decrees, the occupying authorities, the Dépôt, the barracks, History, time—everything that defiles and destroys you—have been able to take away from her. (119)

As this final sentence confirms, Dora's secret, as Modiano imagines it, not only liberates her from all that the nightmare of the Dark Years represents, but also from the weight of the past, from History itself. In understanding this, and in identifying so intensely with her, the novelist experiences Dora's liberation for himself, as his own. It is not surprising, then, that in subsequent works, the Occupation, and all that it represents for Modiano, becomes less of a haunting presence, a dark sun hanging over his fictional world. And with the diminution of the burden of the past, of History itself, a *future* becomes a possible reality.

Before that future is possible, however, another past, Modiano's *roman familial*, must be dealt with and put to rest. And while *Dora Bruder* does not perform or enact a cathartic purge of *that* past, it does make progress toward, and indeed set the stage for it. As *Dora Bruder* confirms again and again, the Occupation and the writer's *roman familial* are inextricably intertwined. Therefore, if Modiano is truly to experience a cathartic liberation from the Dark Years, the issue of his deeply troubled relationship with his parents must be resolved as well.

From the outset of *Dora Bruder*, the writer's *enquête* establishes intimate links between her family and his own, especially where Modiano's father is concerned. Early on, in seeking documentary evidence concerning Dora and her family in the 12th Arrondissement Registry Office, Modiano loses his way in the large building. He panics, and this feeling reminds him of a similar experience twenty years earlier when he had got lost in the Pitié-Saltpétrière trying to find his father, who was hospitalized there. Later, he imagines that the girl his father told him he had ridden with in the police paddy wagon during the Occupation had been Dora, who was on one of her fugues (51). Like Modiano's father, Dora was not registered in the 1940 census of

Jews; unlike him, she did not become an outlaw and black marketeer living as a Jew during the Occupation. Nor, of course, did she survive it, as he had.

Perhaps the strongest connection between Dora's family and Modiano's concerns the characters of the two fathers and their relationship with their respective children. Although the nature of the connection—the two pairs are essentially opposites—is not fully apparent until *Un pedigree*, *Dora Bruder* establishes the ground for this contrast. First, there is a fundamental *goodness* and honor to Ernst Bruder (according to his niece's testimony cited earlier), and he is to all appearances deeply devoted to his daughter.[17] The documentary evidence assembled, fragmentary as it is, strongly suggests this. As noted earlier, Modiano writes of Dora's father's inability to get off work to be present at the registry of her birth. In his account of Ernst Bruder's past, he also stresses the hardships he endured in postwar Vienna, where there was not enough to eat. The writer then emphasizes the danger of life in the Foreign Legion and the homesickness Bruder must have felt for Vienna while in the deserts of North Africa. Similarly, the novelist imagines Dora's father's anxieties about whether and when to alert the police after she had run away from school and disappeared. Concerning the thirteen "long" days he waited before going to the police, Modiano stresses Ernst Bruder's "anguish and indecision," especially in light of the fact that, by "trying to find her, he was drawing attention to her" (62).

It is important to emphasize that it is the writer's empathetic imagination that makes of Ernst Bruder a simple, good, and honorable man. In reality, Modiano can only surmise that Bruder could not be present at the registry of Dora's birth because of apparent difficult working conditions. Modiano can also ultimately only deduce the wretchedness of Bruder's existence in Vienna, or intuit Bruder's longing for the beauties of his homeland while fighting in the desert. The "anguish and indecision" Bruder felt while waiting to report Dora's disappearance to the police is certainly logical and plausible, but there are other possible interpretations of Bruder's delay. As the text makes clear, a less charitable reading would be that Ernst Bruder resisted notifying the police out of fear for his own safety. In any

---

17. Modiano's interest in a devoted Jewish father and his wayward or troubled daughter dates back, of course, to the 1974 film *Lacombe Lucien*, the script for which Modiano co-wrote with Louis Malle.

case, Modiano's empathy for Ernst Bruder and his implicit faith in his motives and actions are apparent; his attachment to him is only enhanced by his identification with Dora.

In *Dora Bruder*, Modiano's real father is referred to several times, and the writer's attitude toward him can best be described as ambivalent. In some instances it is neutral, as when he imagines it is Dora whom his father sees across from him in the paddy wagon. In others, the writer expresses a kind of strained sympathy for his father, despite the latter's shortcomings. Pointing out that, unlike Dora, his father had survived through crime, Modiano nevertheless justifies his father's actions: "since they had made him an outlaw, he had no choice but to follow that same course, to live on his wits in Paris and vanish into the swamps of the black market" (52). Later, he acknowledges that in writing *La place de l'étoile* he had wanted to get back at those literary anti-Semites who "by insulting my father, had wounded me. And on the terrain of French prose to silence them once and for all" (58).

But it is precisely in the context of Modiano's statement about the inspiration for *La place de l'étoile* that the writer's apparent façade of empathy and sympathy for his father crumbles. Writing about his father's hostility toward him, Modiano states that his father had no qualms in causing his son to experience the same feelings of fear and humiliation he himself had experienced during the Occupation. In a scene as remarkable for its cruelty, if not as dire in its outcome, as the arrest of Dora and other Jews during the Occupation, Modiano describes his father denouncing him to the police, having him arrested, and taken away in a paddy wagon because Modiano had demanded that his father pay the child support he owed. After describing this event, the writer adds that, a year later, his father hid his son's military call-up papers so that he would be taken away by force to do his military service. But then suddenly—and incongruously—Modiano refers again to his orchestrated arrest and states: "I bore him no grudge" (58).

This passage marks the last substantive mention of Modiano's father in *Dora Bruder*. It is also the only passage in the book in which the destructive and traumatic potential of his father's emotional violence toward him is fully exposed. Modiano can only begin to grasp the extent of his father's antipathy and articulate the truth of their relationship by viewing both through the illuminating lens of his identification with Dora: Ernst Bruder leads him to understand and appreciate what a kind and devoted father can be. And yet, at this moment of real insight, Modiano draws back from this painful realization when he states that he bears his father "no grudge." So while a cathartic liberation from the horror of the Dark Years through Dora and her story is possible in *Dora Bruder*, Modiano is not yet able to rid himself of the full weight of his troubled familial past. That task, it appears, will require another eight years, and will be finally realized in *Un pedigree*.

That *Un pedigree* is essentially in dialogue with *Dora Bruder*, that it constitutes in some ways a completion of the earlier work is evident, first, in the documentary, "investigative" tone and content of many of its passages. Modiano describes it as "a simple film of deeds and facts" (41). But *Un pedigree* also takes up, "fills in," or revises historical strands woven into the fabric of *Dora Bruder*, while adding historical details of its own. For example, in the first pages of *Un pedigree*, Modiano returns to his father's wartime career: his failure to register as a Jew with the authorities, his black marketeering, and his February 1942 arrest and trip to police headquarters in a paddy wagon. In *Un pedigree*, however, he provides additional details about the arrest: Albert Modiano was arrested with his Jewish German girlfriend Helga H. (a former fiancée of Billy Wilder) and when he arrives at the police station is taken before Superintendent Schweblin. Modiano's readers have already encountered Schweblin and his men in *Dora Bruder* as the brutal plunderers of Jewish possessions as their owners are about to be deported. And in *Dora Bruder*, Modiano recalls that his father remembers seeing Schweblin in postwar Paris, even though he was supposed to have been "disposed of" by the Germans in 1943. In *Un pedigree* the reader also learns of his mother's politically dubious past during the Occupation: her work for German-owned Continental Films, her friendship with the actress Arletty, whose own wartime career landed her in hot water at the Liberation, and so on.

But unlike in *Dora Bruder*, the horror of the Dark Years and the scandal of French complicity in the Holocaust are not the ultimate stakes, the "antagonists" of *Un pedigree*. Rather, these stakes concern his mother (less centrally, as it turns out), his father, and ultimately, the enigma of the person of the writer himself. In coming to terms with both parents over the course of the episodes and events recounted, the writer is finally able to achieve a form of tragic clarity, completing the cathartic process begun in *Dora Bruder*.

By the end of *Un pedigree*, the episodes recalled about Modiano's mother add up to a simple and harsh truth, announced early on: his mother was "a pretty girl with an arid heart" (3). Nothing recounted subsequently in Modiano's memoir changes or nuances this perception. If anything, later episodes confirm that she was a superficial person, as well as politically and morally suspect. Modiano is somewhat circumspect about her youth and arrival in Paris, but the implications are clear in the details he provides. She leaves her native Belgium because her fiancé's parents do not want him to marry her. Why, the reader is not told. She arrives in Paris through the good graces of an officer in the Propaganda-Staffel, and there consorts with German soldiers and collaborators, not to mention black marketeers, like Modiano *père*. After the war, and throughout Modiano's youth, she is an inconstant and frequently mercenary presence. At one point, she lives with him off of his meager allowance from his father. At another, she pockets, "steely-eyed," the two hundred francs he gets for pawning a pen he had won for literary prize (91). She also offers him poor advice. On the recommendation of a friend, she tells her son to read Montherlant, because he is "full of good advice" about how to "act around women" (71–72). Even the young Modiano recognizes the dubiousness of Montherlant as a role model "in sexual matters," given his misogyny (to put it mildly) in the 1930s quartet of novels, *The Girls*, and, as was later revealed, his voracious, lifelong pederasty.[18] As for her maternal feelings for him, Modiano asserts that he "found no favor in her eyes" (60–61). Later, he adds, "nothing softened the coldness and hostility she had always shown me. I was never able to confide in her or ask her help of any kind" (90). The passage concludes pessimistically with the lament that suffering over her was "suffering for nothing" (91). And while the writer acknowledges "praying to God to forgive her," when going to catechism as a child, and ultimately surviving her cruelty, others were less fortunate or forgiving. Modiano admits to a feeling of strong kinship with his mother's dog, a chow who, ignored by its master, killed itself by jumping from a window.

If coming to terms with his mother's memory means, in the end, "making a simple film of deeds and facts" documenting her cruelty and indifference toward, and exploitation of her son, Modiano's father

18. Along these lines, Montherlant's correspondence with Roger Peyrefitte, published in the 1980s, is particularly illuminating.

in *Un pedigree* is a more complicated case altogether. In the episodes recounted in the memoir, Albert Modiano demonstrates the same remarkable cruelty and indifference toward his son as he did in *Dora Bruder*. Lost and panicked as a youth in London, Modiano calls his father for help, but his father only "wishes [him] good luck in an indifferent voice" (58). Elsewhere, after leaving the dormitories at the Lycée Henri-IV, an act that displeases his father, the latter agrees to meet his son only by appointment and in cafés. Following the paddy wagon episode described in *Dora Bruder*, the father refuses to enter the building where they both live at the same time as his son. Eventually, he demolishes the staircase that had linked his apartment to the one Modiano shared with his mother. In the rubble where the staircase had been, the writer finds childhood books and postcards he had written to his deceased brother, Rudy. They are "torn to pieces," apparently by the father. Later, Modiano describes his father enrolling him without his knowledge in advanced literature courses at a *lycée* in Bordeaux. He then takes him there by train, without luggage, and gives him one hundred and fifty francs to survive on. For the writer, the experience was like "being kidnapped" (103). Near the conclusion of *Un pedigree*, Modiano expands on his account in *Dora Bruder* of his father's efforts to force him into military service. The episode closes with an exchange of letters between father and son— documents similar to the Tartakowsky letter in *Dora Bruder*—which mark the conclusion of a parent/child relationship, only on a very different note. After quoting the letter exchange, Modiano writes: "I never saw him again" (127).

Repellent for the almost surgical cruelty and indifference he shows his son, Albert Modiano's politics, reflected in his friendships and business activities, are hardly less reprehensible. Accounts of his parents' activities during the Occupation lead Modiano to wonder if his father's acquaintances were "police stooges" or "Gestapo henchmen" (21). Later, the writer realizes that a building his father takes him to near the Bois de Boulogne, and which his father apparently knew well, had previously housed the wartime black market Otto Bureau: "And suddenly the stench of rot blends in with the smells of the riding clubs and dead leaves in the Bois [de Boulogne]" (39–40). As if to link his father to the worst political elements and crimes of the Dark Years, Modiano notes that the Ford he'd used for his illicit activities during the war had later been commandeered by the *Milice* to kidnap Georges Mandel, whose "bullet-riddled body" had been found in it.

These aspects of the father's past, his identity, and his dealings with his son are clear—and frankly damning—but the fact that Albert Modiano is Jewish stimulates a more ambivalent response from his son and greatly complicates the writer's attitude toward and feelings about his father. In important ways, it also forces him to confront the enigma of his own existence. Indeed, in the opening paragraph of *Un pedigree*, the writer directly links his father's Jewishness to his own sense of identity—or lack thereof—by acknowledging that he never knew how his father felt about being Jewish and that fact, coupled with the circumstances of his own birth, made him feel like an "illegitimate son" (1). Hence his sense of being without a "pedigree."

Albert's Jewishness forces his son to see him in a more sympathetic light, and even, on occasion, to excuse his actions. At least equally importantly, it also intensifies the mystery that surrounds him—a mystery that is entirely absent from the mother. Modiano attempts to explain his father's inability to settle down, his wanderlust, his "searching for El Dorado, in vain":

> I wonder whether he wasn't trying to flee the Occupation years. He never told me what he felt, deep inside, in Paris during that period. Fear? The strange sensation of being hunted simply because someone had classified him as a specific type of prey, when he didn't really know what he was? (27)

Later, after seeing with his father images of the death camps in a German film on Nuremberg entitled *Hitler's Executioners*, the writer acknowledges: "Something changed in my life that day." He adds: "And what did my father think? We never talked about it, not even as we left the theater" (54). All that Modiano is able to surmise after seeing a book on his father's bedside table entitled *How to Make Friends* is that his father was intensely alone, largely as a result of his experiences as a Jew during the Occupation. But, as Modiano acknowledges near the beginning of *Un pedigree*, his father "took his secrets to the grave" (14).

Unlike the majority of Modiano's fictional protagonists and narrators, in *Un pedigree* the writer is overtly fraught with anguish. Indeed, the intensity of the writer's emotions is such that in certain instances he tends to deny them altogether. In other instances he acknowledges, or at least implies, that the process of writing the story is itself painful. Finally, toward the end of *Un pedigree*, he confesses his wish that everything could have been different with his parents.

On the first score, in a poignant passage that the memoir itself ultimately belies, Modiano writes: "Apart from my brother, Rudy, his death, I don't believe that anything I relate here truly matters to me . . . I have nothing to confess or elucidate and I have no interest in soul-searching or self-reflection" (41). Virtually everything he recounts about his relations with his parents in *Un pedigree*, as well as other aspects of the memoir, contradict these claims.

Several comments throughout the book reveal that the process of writing it was extremely difficult. This is especially the case late in the memoir, when the weight of his parents' transgressions and the writer's consequent loneliness become increasingly hard for him to bear. Just before describing his stay as a boarding student at the Lycée Henri-IV, Modiano writes: "It's not my fault if the words jumble together. I have to move more quickly, before I lose heart." In his final reflections on his increasingly difficult relations with his father and mother, Modiano admonishes himself: "Let's be honest to the bitter end" (120). At the same time, he expresses the desire to go back and "relive those years better than I lived them then." In one of the more touching passages in the memoir, Modiano writes that, if his father had known him after his literary success, things would have been very different:

> If he'd known me ten years later . . . there wouldn't have been the slightest problem between us. He would have enjoyed talking literature to me, I could have asked him about his financial dealings and mysterious past. And so, in another life, we walk arm in arm, not hiding our meetings from anyone. (126)

The key words are "another life." The reality, described in the memoir's next paragraph, is that the exchange of letters between father and son brought an abrupt and brutal end to their relationship.

Given these circumstances—the utter failure of the writer's relationship with his parents and the death of his brother—how is catharsis possible? What form can it take, and how might it mark a "completion" of the cathartic moment that concludes *Dora Bruder*? In *Dora Bruder*, it is the discovery of the young Jewish girl's secret, the secret of her flights from Catholic boarding school, that offer a form of redemption and catharsis for her, and perhaps more so for the writer. In Modiano's eyes, it frees her memory from the weight of History, and of France's Dark Years in particular. In *Un pedigree*, the pursuit of his father's "secret," his mysterious experiences during the Occupation, is also at the heart of the writer's—his son's—quest. But unlike in *Dora Bruder*, where we learn at the *conclusion* of the work of the redemptive nature of Dora's "poor and precious" secret, in *Un pedigree* we learn of the failure of the quest at the outset: early on, Modiano tells us that his father "took his secrets to the grave" (14). Nonetheless, in the process of seeking to learn the truth about his father's past in *Un pedigree*, Modiano discovers another mystery that, as painful as it is, ultimately proves illuminating—and cathartic. Near the conclusion of the memoir, the writer realizes that what sums up his sad misadventures with his father is the latter's "mysterious compulsion always to push me away: schools, Bordeaux, the police station, the army" (122). This "mysterious compulsion" is ultimately his father's "secret." It is not a "presence," but an "absence," an absence of love, an indifference that ultimately accounts for his cruelty and neglect. Moreover, as *Un pedigree* shows, this absence and indifference are shared by both parents. Just as through writing *Dora Bruder* Modiano discovers Dora's "secret," by literally forcing himself to write *Un pedigree*, he discovers the "secret," he solves the riddle of his troubled, traumatic relations with his parents. In the technical terms of catharsis cited earlier, Modiano eliminates "the complex by bringing it to consciousness and affording it expression." He can finally move on. So it is perhaps appropriate that the cathartic moment in *Un pedigree* occurs when his vocation as a *writer* is validated with the acceptance of his first novel for publication. Modiano writes: "I felt unburdened for the first time in my life. The threat that had weighed on me for so many years, kept me on edge, had dissolved in the Paris air. I had set sail before the worm-eaten wharf could collapse. It was time" (130).

TO THE FUTURE

If *Dora Bruder* and *Un pedigree* together form an exercise in catharsis, a purging of historical and familial trauma, an "illumination" turning "a painful story into a profound and moving experience," what might this achievement mean for Modiano's subsequent work? To be sure in books such as *Paris Nocturne*, *In the Café of Lost Youth*, *So You Don't Get Lost in the Neighborhood*, the Dark Years of the Occupation and the Holocaust are not the central historical backdrop. Nor do troubled relations with parents like those found in Modiano's earlier works haunt the protagonists and the texts themselves. But in one work in particular, the 2010 novel *L'horizon*, perhaps the extent of the writer's catharsis, his liberation, is most clearly—if obliquely—revealed. *L'horizon* focuses on the love affair between a certain Bosmans and a German girl, Margaret le Coz. It combines many of the usual elements of a Modiano novel: menacing, mysterious figures (Margaret is stalked by Boyaval, and she is forced to flee regularly to new cities and hide under pseudonyms to avoid him); a protagonist haunted by people and episodes from his youth, and so on. Bosmans is also tailed as a young man by an old woman and her partner, who demand his money whenever they catch up with him. He confesses to Margaret one night that the woman is "my mother, if I believe my identity papers" (38). And he has no idea why she and her partner show him "so much disdain" (39). Readers of *Un pedigree* will of course recognize the writer's own mother as the inspiration for Bosman's, but there is an important difference between the two. In *L'horizon* Bosman's mother, frightening though she may be, is reduced to a caricature, a quasi-comic presence who, in the end, only forces her son to flee her on the street. She has no real, emotional hold over him, nor is she ultimately a menace to him.

Unlike so many love affairs in Modiano's works, *L'horizon* concludes *not* with the protagonist's beloved lost forever, but with Bosmans in Berlin about to find Margaret again years later in the bookshop she owns. The future—the "horizon" of the title—is for once in sight, and the past is reconciled: "[Bosmans] experienced for the first time a feeling of serenity, with the certitude of having returned to the exact place from which he had departed one day, at the same hour and in the same season, as the two hands of the clock come together on the clock face at noon" (171). As the last line of *Un pedigree* states: "It was time."

LYNN A. HIGGINS

Modiano at the Movies[1]

What can we learn from Patrick Modiano's lifelong enthusiasm for
the cinema? Although he pledges allegiance exclusively to the novel,
his fondness for movies is multi-faceted and far-reaching. His most
substantial contribution is, of course, his script for Louis Malle's controversial 1974 film, *Lacombe Lucien*. Modiano also co-wrote screen-
plays for several less familiar productions, among them Jean-Paul
Rappeneau's Occupation comedy, *Bon voyage* (2003) and Pascal Au-
bier's family drama, *Le fils de Gascogne* (1996). The writer also col-
laborated in adapting several of his novels, most notably *Le parfum
d'Yvonne* (1993, directed by Patrice Leconte, from *Villa triste*) and
Manuel Poirier's *Te Quiero* (2001, from *Dimanches d'août*). Modiano
has suggested that movies have served him as a refuge and a reservoir
of ideas;[2] his novels and interviews contain a wealth of cinematic
references. And yet, perhaps because the evidence of it is so scattered,
his involvement with cinema has received surprisingly little critical
comment. An exception is a 2006 article in which Colin Nettelbeck
offers a valuable overview of cinematic narrative techniques that
the novelist has adapted for the purposes of narrative fiction. Nettelbeck concludes by asserting that Modiano's unique writing practice
brings the resources of cinematic storytelling to enrich and renew the
French novelistic tradition.[3]

1. My thinking about this essay has been enriched by conversations with Sam Di
Iorio, Richard J. Golsan, Thomas Pillard, Phil Powrie, Henry Rousso, Maurice Samuels,
Susan Suleiman, and Steven Ungar.
    2. "Ce que je dois au cinéma," in *Modiano*, ed. Maryline Heck and Raphaëlle
Guidée (Paris: Cahiers de L'Herne, 2012), 235–43.
    3. Colin Nettelbeck, "Modiano's Style: A Novelist in the Age of Cinema," *French
Cultural Studies* 17/1 (February 2006): 35–54.

YFS 133, *"Detecting" Patrick Modiano*, ed. Golsan and Higgins, © 2018 by Yale University.

While these approaches offer valuable insights, my question lies elsewhere: ultimately, I want to know how Modiano's immersion in cinema has shaped his understanding of history. In order to approach that question, I examine two of his novels and, in each case, map a path from a specific movie to the evocations of World War II and the German Occupation for which Modiano is deservedly famous.

It is not difficult to document Modiano's early interest in cinema. As a teenager, he was a regular moviegoer and took copious notes, for example on Pabst's *Loulou*.[4] He discussed *Thunder in the Sun* with Raymond Queneau, an acquaintance of his mother's, who became his mentor. His characters follow sensational news stories *(faits divers)* involving movie stars such as Lana Turner, Marilyn Monroe, and Errol Flynn. The young Modiano also worked briefly collecting background materials for Jacques Audiard. In novels and interviews, he regularly describes reality as if it were a film, for example: "Until I was twenty-one years old, I lived the events of my life in rear-screen transparency projection—a process that consists of projecting the moving landscape as a backdrop, while the characters sit motionless on a studio set."[5] He self-deprecatingly compares his own exaggerated gesticulations to Jacques Tati's Monsieur Hulot.[6] And when his protagonists undertake those typical Modianesque urban rambles on the trail of some enigma or missing person, they always note the location of existing and former movie houses. In 2000, Modiano served on the jury of the Cannes Film Festival. He even makes one of his first-person narrators into a filmmaker.[7] Immersed in cinema, then.

That young Patrick acquired his affinity for movies from both sides of his family adds emotional weight to his cinephilia. His mother, Louisa Colpijn (or Colpeyn), initially established herself as a minor starlet in her native Belgium before she followed the advice of a German officer friend and moved to Paris in 1941, at the age of twenty-three, to take a job dubbing films into Flemish for the Nazi-created production company, Continental Films. She also pursued a career

4. "Notes sur *Loulou* de Pabst," in *Modiano* (Cahiers de L'Herne), 258–64. (Modiano originally took those notes in 1960, when he was 15.) *Loulou* (1929) is also known as *Pandora's Box*.

5. Patrick Modiano, *Un pedigree* (Paris: Gallimard, 2005), 109, 45. All translations here are my own unless otherwise noted.

6. *Patrick Modiano: Je me souviens de tout. . .*, a documentary about Modiano written by Bernard Pivot and directed by Antoine de Meaux (Paris: Gallimard, 2015), DVD.

7. A documentary filmmaker, in *Voyage de noces* (Paris: Gallimard, 1990).

acting on the Parisian stage and on tour, leaving her two young sons with acquaintances. After the Liberation, she landed supporting movie roles playing Russian countesses and other similar characters, where her noticeable foreign accent was an asset.

In the early 1960s, the teenage Patrick became a habitué of the Cinémathèque, where he discovered the pre-war classics of Poetic Realism and saw all the *Nouvelle vague* films as soon as they were released. He also enjoyed first-hand encounters with several of the New Wave's luminaries, including Catherine Deneuve, whose father, Maurice Dorléac, figured among his mother's theater contacts. Modiano and Deneuve would later co-author a book in memory of Deneuve's sister, Françoise Dorléac. Modiano would even eventually play a small role alongside Deneuve in Raùl Ruiz's *Généalogies d'un crime* (1997). Modiano's mother was also friendly with Anna Karina, who encouraged her to accept a small role in Godard's *Bande à part*. Modiano reports that the actors and crew showed up unexpectedly one day at his mother's apartment on the Quai de Conti to shoot a scene from his bedroom window![8]

As for the paternal contribution to Modiano's cinema education, one can understand why among the New Wave films, young Patrick identified particularly strongly with Truffaut's *Les 400 coups*. Its hero, Antoine Doinel, was his own age when the film appeared, and he, like the young Modiano, ran away from the school where he had been unwillingly enrolled, and who suffered episodes of paternal neglect and abuse like Modiano. Patrick and a half-dozen of his fictional avatars see their fathers only rarely, but when they do, the father invariably takes his son to a picture show. Sometimes it is suggested that Albert Modiano is hiding from the police, but perhaps he simply didn't know how else to entertain his strange, introspective son. In his autobiographical *Un pédigree*, Modiano recounts that in 1958, when he was thirteen, his father took him to see a newly released German documentary, *The Nuremberg Trial*, which included images of the Nazi extermination camps. "Something changed for me that day," he declares.[9]

At age sixteen, Modiano dreamed of owning a magically invisible lightweight camera that would make it possible to record faces and conversations in the streets, ideally without requiring film at all, or

8. "Ce que je dois au cinéma," 235.
9. *Un pedigree*, 56–57.

if so, only a film stock so sensitive it could simply absorb life directly ["une pellicule si sensible qu'elle se serait laissée tout simplement imprégner par la vie"[10]]. Instead of choosing a career in cinema, however, movies served him primarily as what he calls a "laboratoire romanesque." Given his immersion in film culture, it stands to reason that his novels would be infused with what could be called a cinematic imaginary. We might borrow the term "cinepoetics" from Christophe Wall-Romana's study of cinema's impact on French Modernist poetry to describe the way a writer can *think literature through film*. Cinepoetics is defined as "a writing practice whose basic process is homological: it consists of envisioning a specific aspect or component of poetry as if it were a specific component of cinema." The theory encompasses the adaptation of cinematic techniques to writing, but it also entails a broader adoption of a cinematic worldview, a process of "reassess[ing] the articulation of meaning with embodiment and technology."[11]

We can now consider two instances where cinema functions as a narrative template and a fantasmatic universe that modulates how Modiano figures himself, the world, and the historical past.

Dora Bruder recounts a quest by a narrator (Modiano himself) to reconstruct the experiences of a fifteen-year-old Jewish girl during the summer of 1941, from her disappearance (her *fugue*) from the convent where she had been placed in hiding until her arrest by the Nazis several months later. She was subsequently deported to Auschwitz, where she died. As this narrator tries to reconstruct the young runaway's itinerary, he crisscrosses Paris, visiting sites where Dora's presence was documented, including her home address, the hospital where she was born, the school she probably attended, and the metro stations and streets she must have taken to get there. He consults old phone books and weather records from the months when she was at large in the city. What he is unable to reconstruct from documents, he tries to deduce. This is where his cinematic imagination kicks in.

Among the sources Modiano consults is *Premier rendez-vous*, a romantic comedy released in Paris theaters on August 14, 1941, that is to say, during the period when Dora's whereabouts were unknown. The film was directed by Henri Decoin for Continental Films, the

10. "La caméra légère," *Modiano* (Cahiers de L'Herne), 265–66 (orig. 1999).
11. Christophe Wall-Romana, *Cinepoetry: Imaginary Cinemas in French Poetry* (New York: Fordham UP, 2015), 3, 6, 8.

production company launched by Joseph Goebbels less than a year previously and presided over by Alfred Greven. (It was also, perhaps not incidentally, the company where Modiano's mother had taken a job after her arrival in Paris earlier that same year.)

Premier rendez-vous portrays a teenage orphan, Micheline (Danielle Darrieux), who escapes from an orphanage to meet a stranger with whom she has corresponded through a lovelorn column in *Paris-Soir* and whom she imagines to be a dashing young movie star. But when her secret admirer—a lonely but harmless middle-aged literature teacher—discovers how young and naïve she is, he scrupulously pretends to be standing in for his young protégé, Pierre (Louis Jourdan). Once she meets Pierre, Micheline adroitly overcomes his initial resistance, wins his heart, and all ends happily: the teacher's entire class is enlisted to raid the orphanage and he officially adopts Micheline in order to set her free. Here's how Dora Bruder's narrator describes this film:

> In the summer of 1941, one of the films made under the Occupation, first shown at the Normandy Theater, came to the neighborhood cinemas. It was a harmless comedy: *Premier rendez-vous*. The last time I saw it, I had a strange feeling, out of keeping with the thin plot and the sprightly tone of the actors. I told myself that perhaps, one Sunday, Dora Bruder had been to see this film, whose subject was a girl her age who runs away. [. . .] During her flight, as in fairy tales and romances, she meets her Prince Charming. This film paints a rosy, anodyne picture of what had happened to Dora in real life. Did it give her the idea of running away?[12]

The "strange feeling" that the film provoked can be explained by the many details of *Premier rendez-vous* that correspond uncannily to the bits of Dora's story our narrator has already pieced together. Micheline meets her admirer through the same newspaper to which the Bruder parents will submit a desperate missing-person announcement some six months later; she escapes from an orphanage that the narrator supposes must resemble the convent school from which Dora ran away. Glued to the screen, he scrutinizes details of the dormitory, the corridors, the school uniforms, the café where the heroine waits after nightfall, and he imagines Dora into the film's décor. Micheline

---

12. *Dora Bruder*, trans. Joanna Kilmartin (U. California Press, 1999), 65. (Orig. Gallimard, 1997). I have made corrections here to Kilmartin's translation. Further references in this article are to this translation.

is as insouciant, rebellious, and unaware of the risks she is taking as he guesses Dora to have been. (Micheline might also be a model for the young Jewish girl, France, in *Lacombe Lucien*.) Did our narrator recognize Dora's story in Micheline's, or did Micheline's story provide him with a template and an inspiration to flesh out Dora's story?

Despite its lighthearted plot, *Premier rendez-vous* is saturated with an aura of clandestinity and foreboding. Micheline disguises herself as a boy in order to venture outdoors and panics when she sees a policeman. Her protector hurries to close the window, lest her singing be overheard. She knows that if she is captured, she will be sent to a reformatory. Eventually, the headmistress catches sight of Micheline and has her arrested; this moment of spectatorship must have been overwhelming in the way it condenses into one nightmarish scene traumatic incidents suffered by Micheline, Dora, Antoine Doinel, Modiano's father, and Modiano himself.[13]

Our narrator mentions that *Premier rendez-vous* first appeared at the *Normandie* cinema house. Now the *UGC Normandie* on the Champs Elysées, the theater was, during the Occupation, a privileged venue for German officers. It is appalling to imagine the risks Dora would have run had she hazarded to see the movie there (which is unlikely). One can only hope she saw it—if indeed she did see it—in the cinema next to her home. (The narrator recognized Dora's address in the newspaper notice, because he knew the movie theater next door.) Modiano's experience of the movie was also undoubtedly inflected by the fact that Louis Jourdan subsequently became somewhat of a Resistance hero (and even later played Pierre Mendès-France in a TV series), while Danielle Darrieux was criticized by the public and targeted by the Resistance after touring Germany during the Occupation.

Although the characters remain oblivious to historical events, and there are no backgrounded German uniforms or portraits of Pétain, the film itself announces its precise time frame by means of a montage of calendar pages marking the days from May 26 to June 3, 1941. Given these unobtrusive but explicit clues, contemporary audiences could not possibly have missed the coded language in one critical scene. When the orphanage headmistress becomes aware of Micheline's disappearance, she grills the other girls and then assures them in menacing tones that the runaway *will* be apprehended: "We

---

13. And Alfred Hitchcock, too, as Modiano notes in his 2014 Nobel acceptance speech.

will capture her," she declares. "She won't get far, you can be sure of that, young ladies. Without money, without identity papers, and with clothing that gives you away [avec un costume qui vous dénonce], there's no chance in the world that she can escape." Literally a reference to Micheline's convent school uniform, the conspicuously generalized "costume qui vous dénonce" can easily be understood to evoke the yellow star that Dora was required to wear (but didn't wear) on her lapel, *la place de l'étoile.*

Modiano's narrator is aware that other moviegoers of Dora's time might also not have survived the war, and he describes how during the Occupation (and for young runaways of any era), the cinema served as a place of refuge, where one could be surrounded by others in protective anonymity. He imagines their feelings in such vivid detail that we should thus not be overly surprised that the details of Dora's story, as he reconstructs it, come to align closely with Micheline's. Here, he introduces a startling idea:

> Suddenly, I realized that this film was impregnated with the gazes of moviegoers [**imprégné** par les regards des spectateurs] from the time of the Occupation [. . .] And, by some kind of chemical process, all those gazes had materially altered the actual film [avaient modifié la substance même de la **pellicule**], the lighting, the voices of the actors. That is what I had sensed, thinking of Dora Bruder and faced with the ostensibly trivial images of *Premier rendez-vous*" (66, orig. 80, emphasis added).

This fanciful reverie echoes the young Modiano's dream of a magical camera with "une **pellicule** si sensible qu'elle se serait laissée tout simplement **imprégner** par la vie." Etymologically, *pellicule* means *petite peau* or little skin; thus, as he watches *Premier rendez-vous* while worrying about Dora, the narrator is able to palpably and imaginatively reach through the film/*pellicule* to make direct contact with her.

For Modiano, streets, buildings, objects—and, it turns out, a film—can function as privileged repositories of memory. But this fantasy of "skin-to-skin" access to the physical reality of the past is both more and other than a memory: it is a way of harnessing cinema's power to resurrect the past *in the present*. Within the logic of this fantasy, our narrator seeks not so much to remember as to re-animate; film is not as much a *lieu de mémoire* as it is a site of incarnation—the way actors "incarnate" roles on the screen—and even of re-incarnation.

Here we can sense Modiano's cinepoetic imagination striving to "[re-assess] the articulation of meaning with embodiment and technology." Media are part of our consciousness. Memories of movies are . . . memories. A film can make it possible to relive the sensations and emotions surrounding past events and put yourself empathically into the skin of others, including those you never knew. The encounter with Dora Bruder through *Premier rendez-vous* shows us exactly how knowledge of the past can be mediated by movies. This power that cinema exerts could thus well lie behind Modiano's oft-repeated claim that he retains memories from the time of the Occupation, which ended before he was born.

REMEMBERING "LES ANNÉES NOIRES"

In the wake of his 2014 Nobel Prize, Modiano told an interviewer that he got the idea for *Rue des boutiques obscures* (1978), one of his most beloved early novels and a winner of the Prix Goncourt, from a Hollywood movie, *Somewhere in the Night*, a classic *film noir* directed by Joseph Mankiewicz and released in 1946.[14] That film begins in a military hospital, where a heavily bandaged man regains consciousness after extensive plastic surgery, with no recollection of who he is. His only clues are a wallet that tells him his name may be George Taylor, and a note from one Larry Cravat, possibly a business associate. Leaving the hospital, George heads to Los Angeles to recover his own past by tracking down this Larry Cravat. With help from a nightclub singer he meets by chance, George will eventually recover a suitcase full of Nazi cash that he had apparently stashed away before his departure for the war.

Like George Taylor, the protagonist of *Rue des boutiques obscures* suffers from amnesia following some trauma he does not remember. An actual professional gumshoe, he adopts the name "Guy Roland" and sets out to discover what happened and who he is. Although he eventually pieces together (or imagines) details of an ill-fated escape across a border, his investigation, too, generates danger, anxiety, and plot twists, while raising more questions than it answers. But whereas the Hollywood hero resolves his questions, wins the girl, finds the loot, and gets away, Guy Roland is less successful.

14. Anka Muhlstein, "Did Patrick Modiano Deserve It?" *The New York Review of Books*, December 18, 2014. http://www.nybooks.com/articles/2014/12/18/did-patrick-modiano-deserve-it/.

The most satisfying film adaptations, Modiano believes, are those that have at most a "secret relation" to their source, and in which a director finds in this source something that engages his own obsessions.[15] Although adapted in the opposite direction—film to novel—*Rue des boutiques obscures* uses Mankiewicz's film as a launching pad for its own fiction. Although the novel contains few references to the Occupation, Modiano's familiar themes—his obsessions—are fully engaged: his hero's repressed traumatic past leads to a quest for a missing person through a murky but alluring underworld.

While *Rue des boutiques obscures* overflows with precise visual details, we should nevertheless avoid exaggerating the role of the sense of sight in creating Modiano's fictional world or the novelist's debt to Mankiewicz's film. Guy Roland's most reliable clues are olfactory (a lingering perfume, for example) and auditory (a jazz tune heard from a distant nightclub). Sight is more often invoked to depict atmospherics, such as fog, darkness in a stairway, or the shadowy outline of a face. In interviews, Modiano uses the word "vision" as a synonym for "imagination," and more than one of his protagonists close their eyes in order to "see" better. In their desperate quest to answer questions—What happened? Who am I?—sight is in fact the least reliable of the senses as far as gleaning information is concerned. In short, Modiano's sensibility is more visionary than visual.

Two of his other books explicitly confirm this subordination of vision to the work of the imagination. Both use images and the visible world as points of departure—what the New Novelists of the 1950s and 1960s called "generators"—for writing. *Catherine Certitude* is a charming tale for children and adults about a little girl who discovers that when life gets dull, or when she prefers to ignore her father's pompous and boring business partner, all she has to do is remove her eyeglasses. This gesture opens access to an unsuspected fourth dimension: with glasses, she can see "the world as it is." Without them, she can enter at will into an alternative universe that is "*flou*"—warm and fuzzy, a bit like Sempé's water colors that illustrate the book,[16] and very much like the visual world of Guy Roland. Blurring her sense of sight allows her to detect the gaps in reality and make herself receptive to messages from other senses.

15. Judith Louis, "Voir/Adapter: Entretien avec Patrick Modiano," *Synopsis: Le magazine du scénario* 10 (Nov-Dec 2000): 49.
16. Gallimard, 1988.

In *Paris tendresse*, Brassaï's photographs from the 1930s and 1940s serve as points of departure for Modiano's fanciful riffs about the lives of picturesque strangers, along with echoes from people, places, and ambiences that no longer exist. An accordion player, street acrobats, and a poster of Marlene Dietrich jostle alongside mobilization notices, images of bombed and crumbling buildings, and crowds climbing atop the lion statue at the Place Denfert to welcome American troops. A man seen from behind reminds him of his father. A barge (not pictured) arrives from Belgium; perhaps it's his mother traveling to Paris aboard the *Atalante*. . . .[17]

What these two books share with Modiano's novels is their foregrounding not of how the world *looks*, but of how the seen world makes you *feel*. Images, like other evocative objects, no matter how precisely described, are no more than pre-texts or vehicles for exploration of emotions. For Modiano, unlike a filmmaker, a novelist must work to create a "feeling of uncertainty [une sensation d'incertitude]."[18] This would suggest his descriptive minutiae serve not as a clear visual representation of the world but as a means of teasing out evanescent traces of moods and atmospheres, much like the urban strolls of the *flâneurs* or the Situationist *dérives*.

In short, Modiano's imagination is launched from a particular dimension of *Somewhere in the Night*: its qualities as a *film noir*. Neither a genre nor a movement, *noir* can be identified by standard elements of plot, acting, and *mise-en-scène*, but mostly as style, ambience, mood. Considering *Rue des boutiques obscures* as part of a *film noir* tradition brings into focus certain Modianesque signature motifs in a configuration that is more readily associated with movies than with novels: sketchy night-time scenes set in nightclubs, sleazy walk-ups with neon signs whose effect is heightened by rain or fog; flash-back first-person narration; ambiguous women and vaguely menacing male figures. Modiano himself once remarked that he had been haunted by "American *films noirs* in which there are always identity problems and flashbacks."[19] His affinity for *noir* is further revealed by the specific films he mentions most readily: Marcel Carné's *Quai des brumes* (1938), Orson Welles's *Lady from Shanghai* (1947), Carol Reed's *The Third Man* (1949), Jacques Becker's *Touchez pas au*

---

17. Brassaï and Modiano, *Paris* tendresse (Paris: Éditions Hoëbeke, 1990).
18. Louis, 50.
19. Ibid., 51.

grisbi (1954). His adaptation of *Somewhere in the Night* (1946) reveals that his writing shares a *noir* worldview, a perspective that in turn shapes his representations of the past.

Each attribute of *film noir* that Modiano deploys in his novels merits a chapter of its own, but I want to linger for a moment on one aspect that is both central to his novelistic universe and also quintessentially cinematic: the use of lighting effects. Once one thinks in terms of *film noir*, the sheer magnitude of Modiano's attentiveness to lighting becomes inescapable. His adolescent notes on Pabst's *Loulou*, for example, tell next to nothing about the story and focus only on atmospheric effects. He describes a foggy night scene with threatening but intriguing figures lurking in the shadows. (*"Ombres"* is a favorite word.) He notices a shot of a dark face in a mirror illuminated by a "clarté surnaturelle," a hat that partly shades a face, the melodramatic effect of partially closed shutters.[20] Nearly every page of *Rue des boutiques obscures* contains a reference to how scenes are lit: vapor rising from a street made visible by a dim amber glow; a *minuterie*; silhouettes of dancers against a lighted window; the white outline of a man's coat receding in a darkened stairwell. And in a Proustian moment, the gesture of turning a light switch on and off reminds Guy of something, but what? He recalls vague shapes from a movie seen long ago, but all he retains is the brightness of a sled in the snow. (Is it *Citizen Kane*? *Spellbound*?) In the midst of all this, the mysterious and melancholy obscurity of a restaurant where the music of a zither can be heard makes me wonder whether Guy Roland isn't perhaps *The Third Man*.

Modiano confides in an interview that he has transcribed things he has really experienced and felt, "but I wanted to make of them a kind of atmosphere, a particular luminosity. [. . .] I was always obsessed in cinema with the cameramen. Lighting interested me. [. . .] When one writes, it is perhaps difficult to translate a peculiar light, but it has always preoccupied me."[21] Elsewhere, he explains that he

20. See note 4. As an assiduous fan of *New Wave* cinema, the teenage Modiano must certainly also have reflected on the playful pastiches of American *noir* in films like Godard's *A bout de soufflé*, Truffaut's *Tirez sur le pianiste*, Melville's *Bob le flambeur*, and Chabrol's *Le beau Serge*.

21. Cited in Anne Gillain, "Aesthetic Affinities: Truffaut, Patrick Modiano, Douglas Sirk," in *A Companion to François Truffaut*, ed. Dudley Andrew and Anne Gillian (Hoboken, NJ: Wiley-Blackwell, 2013): 87 (English translation) and 102 (French original).

begins writing a novel by imagining the lighting, which then gives him the setting. Plot and characters come later.[22]

Ruminating about *Premier rendez-vous*, the romantic comedy Dora Bruder might have seen, her narrator identifies the source of the sinister undertones he senses:

> This film paints a rosy, anodyne picture of what had happened to Dora in real life. [. . .] And yet, I had a sense of unease [*un malaise*]. It stemmed from the film's peculiar luminosity, from the grain of the actual stock [le grain même de la pellicule]. Every image seemed veiled in an arctic whiteness that accentuated the contrasts and sometimes obliterated them. The lighting was at once too bright and too dim, either stifling the voices or making their timbre louder, more disturbing. (65; orig. 80).

"Unease," "disturbing," exaggerated contrasts of brightness and shadow, the aura emanating from qualities of light that bring to his mind the idea that the film stock [the *pellicule*] retains the gaze of past spectators. And it's the moral ambiguities represented by light and shadow, the central defining feature of *film noir*, that guide him to seek Dora—and find her—in the film and in the streets of Paris.

Finally, what could be a better setting for a *film noir* than Pigalle at night? This was a neighborhood where the young Modiano had done a lot of nighttime urban rambling while waiting for his mother at the Théâtre Fontaine, near the Blanche métro stop. Evoking *Touchez pas au grisbi* for comparison, he tells Bernard Pivot about the "fantastique parisien" of these boulevards, describing how the magical neon cabaret signs illuminated his "inner landscape" and inspired his novels. We might conclude that Modiano's widely acknowledged fixation on places could more accurately be understood as a passion for lighting and shadows. Far from being just another add-on element, light and shadow are the very generative principles of his writing.

George Taylor and Guy Roland aren't the only *noir* heroes to suffer from traumatic memory loss. In fact, *Somewhere in the Night*, released in 1946, was part of a recognizable corpus of films widely referred to as "amnesia noir," a grouping of films that emerged during the immediate postwar period[23] and that also includes titles like

---

22. *Patrick Modiano: Je me souviens de tout.*
23. Lists of *films noirs* where amnesia is a prominent theme can be found at imdb.com, FilmsNoir.net [sic], and http://www.criminalelement.com/blogs/2011/04/memento-and-amnesia-noir.

George Marshall's *The Blue Dahlia* (1946), Hitchcock's *Spellbound* (1945), Jacques Tourneur's *Out of the Past* (1947), and Orson Welles's *The Stranger* (1946). Whether the condition is medical, psychiatric, or whether the troubling events have been "forgotten" deliberately, amnesia is a transparent figure for guilt, shame, and a desire to make a new start. When François Mitterrand joined Modiano on Bernard Pivot's television program, *Apostrophes,* in 1978 to discuss *Rue des boutiques obscures* (Yes, really!), the future *Président de la République* remarked that when it comes to the Occupation, we all have amnesia: "Nous sommes tous des amnésiques."[24]

It is important, finally, to recall that *film noir* is a variant of melodrama, where light and shadow have the weight of moral allegory. Peter Brooks traces the roots of the genre back to the Revolutionary era, describing the universe of melodrama as "post-sacred": God has fallen silent, leaving the world opaque and unintelligible. Characters in melodrama hope to find clues that would connect their own lives to a larger pattern or narrative, and strive to find meaning by "extract[ing] the true from the real." Focusing on the melodramatic dimensions of Modiano's *noir* sensibility brings into view his characters' post-lapsarian estrangement from origins, the weight of the past on the present, their *malaise* faced with the thick fog of illegible objects and events that surround them, and their desperate pursuit of clues to decipher whatever moral clarity or twisted logic might lie beneath the cataclysms of history. It's as if they, like Catherine, had removed their glasses. The melodramatic feature missing from his novels, of course, is the dramatic reveal, the solution to the mystery.

Brooks asserts that melodrama "comes into being in a world where the traditional imperatives of truth and ethics have been violently thrown into question." And Thomas Elsaesser points out that melodrama enjoys its greatest popularity in periods of dramatic social upheaval and ideological crisis, because it is able to encode them in a palatable, accessible form.[25] The postwar heyday of melodrama in *film noir*—and perhaps especially its "amnesia *noir*" variant—performed important cultural work on hidden social tensions that had to be addressed obliquely. Whether they are overtly "about" the period or not,

24. *Patrick Modiano: Je me souviens de tout.*
25. Peter Brooks, *The Melodramatic Imagination* (New Haven: Yale UP, 1976); Thomas Elsaesser, "Tales of Sound and Fury: Observations on the Family Melodrama," *Film Genre Reader II,* ed. Barry Keith Grant (Austin: University of Texas Press, 1995), 350–80.

films like *Somewhere in the Night* offered Modiano an ideal vehicle for imagining the moral ambiguities and sinister ambiences of the Occupation. This is the shady universe his father inhabited as an unregistered Jew and black-market deal-broker hiding from the Nazis. We might say that his novels figure the war as *les années "noires"* in more than one sense. In classic melodramatic fashion, social and historical questions are displaced onto or represented through family drama; one gets the impression that if his numerous autobiographical protagonists—such as the one in *Rue des boutiques obscures*—could reconstruct their parents' activities, and with them the full atmosphere of the Occupation, they might understand the whole enigma of the war (and perhaps the universe), and they might finally find out where they came from, what they have done, and who they are.

Contributors

BRUNO BLANCKEMAN is Professor of 20th- and 21st-century literature at the Université de la Sorbonne Nouvelle, Paris 3. He is the author of *Les récits indécidables: Jean Echenoz, Hervé Guibert, Pascal Quignard* (2000); *Les fictions singulières* (2002); *Lire Patrick Modiano* (2009); *Le roman depuis la Révolution Française* (2011); *Pour Éric Chevillard* (with Samoyault, D. Viart, 2014). He has also edited several collective works, including *Narrations d'un nouveau siècle: romans et récits français, 2001–2010* (2013) and *Annie Ernaux, Le temps et la mémoire* (2014). *Le dictionnaire Marguerite Yourcenar* appeared in 2017. With Marc Dambre, he co-directs le CERACC (Champ d'Étude du Récit Actuel et Contemporain, UMR THALIM).

MARY CLAIRE CHAO worked in France as a professional translator from 2010 to 2015. She recently earned her M.A. in French from the University of Kansas.

ELLEN COLLIER is a doctoral student at the University of Kansas and co-editor of the department journal *Chimères*. She teaches French to undergraduate students and is working toward writing a dissertation on the subject of medieval literature and linguistics.

MARC DAMBRE is Professor Emeritus at the Université de la Sorbonne Nouvelle (Paris 3) and a researcher at the UMR 7172 THALIM. Recent books include an edition of the correspondence between Paul Morand and Roger Nimier and a book, *Pour l'engagement critique* (both 2015). He also edited the *Cahier de l'Herne, Roger Nimier* (2012).

VANESSA DORIOTT ANDERSON received her Ph.D. in Romance Studies from Duke in 2012. Her research focuses on the relationship

YFS 133, *"Detecting" Patrick Modiano*, ed. Golsan and Higgins, © 2018 by Yale University.

between first-person narrative and history in twentieth-century French literature. She is a program manager in The Graduate School at North Carolina State University.

RICHARD J. GOLSAN is University Distinguished Professor of French and International Studies at Texas A&M University. He is Director of the France/Texas A&M University Institute (*Centre d'Excellence*) and edits *South Central Review*. His recent books include *The Vichy Past in France Today* and *The Trial that Never Ends*, co-edited with Sarah Misemer. His current research interests include the 1970s and the *mode rétro* and French intellectuals from the 1990s to the present.

MARYLINE HECK is Professor of French contemporary literature at Tours University (France). She has published a monograph on Georges Perec (*Georges Perec: Le corps à la lettre*, 2012) and also works on Patrick Modiano and many other French contemporary writers, with a focus on the political implications of literature and the relations between literature and social sciences. Her edited volumes include: *Cahiers Georges Perec 11* ("*Filiations perecquiennes*" 2011), *Cahier de l'Herne* devoted to Georges Perec (with Christelle Reggiani et Claude Burgelin, 2016); *Cahier de l'Herne* devoted to Patrick Modiano (with Raphaëlle Guidée, 2012); *Écrire le travail au XXIe siècle: quelles implications politiques?* (with Aurélie Adler, 2016). She is also the French translator of Michael Sheringham's monograph *Everyday Life* (2006).

LYNN A. HIGGINS is the Edward Tuck Professor of French Studies at Dartmouth College, where she also teaches Comparative Literature and Film Studies. Her books include *New Novel, New Wave, New Politics: Fiction and the Representation of History in Postwar France* and *Bertrand Tavernier*, and her edited or co-edited volumes include *Rape and Representation* and *Conversations with Bertrand Tavernier*. She is the author of articles on, among others, Irène Némirovsky and Julien Duvivier, Marcel Pagnol, Michael Haneke, feminist comedy, Roland Barthes, and Marguerite Duras. She is currently at work on a book about adaptation and other forms of relation between cinema and literature.

VAN KELLY is Associate Professor of French and Francophone studies at the University of Kansas. He has published articles on René Char, J.-M. G. Le Clézio's novels and short stories, Jorge Semprun's representations of Buchenwald and the Gulag, the poetry of René Daumal and Jude Stéfan, dystopias in Céline and Volodine,

Abel Gance and interwar pacifism, and others. He is also author of the book *Pascalian Fictions: The Absent Agent in Pascal's Pensées*. His current research projects are called "Against the Sense of an Ending: René Char and the Paradoxes of Totality, Combat, and Freedom, 1938–1948" and "Senegalese Cityscapes and Mindscapes: Mapping Interactive Social, Political, and Spiritual Spaces of Dakar and Saint-Louis."

CHRISTINE LORD is a Ph.D. candidate in French at the University of Kansas. Her dissertation focuses on human identity in contact with extraterrestrials, machines, and animals in modern French science fiction literature and film.

GERALD PRINCE is Professor of Romance Languages at the University of Pennsylvania. He is the author of many articles and reviews on narrative theory and on modern (French) literature as well as of several books (including *A Dictionary of Narratology* and *Guide du roman de langue française: 1901–1950*). The general editor of the "Stages" series for the University of Nebraska Press, Prince is working on the second volume of his *Guide du roman* (1951–2000).

SUSAN RUBIN SULEIMAN is the C. Douglas Dillon Research Professor of the Civilization of France and Research Professor of Comparative Literature at Harvard University. Her latest book is *The Némirovsky Question: The Life, Death, and Legacy of a Jewish Writer in 20th-Century France* (2016); other books include *Crises of Memory and the Second World War, Subversive Intent: Gender, Politics, and the Avant-Garde, Risking Who One Is: Encounters with Contemporary Art and Literature*, and the memoir *Budapest Diary: In Search of the Motherbook*. Among collective volumes she has edited are *Exile and Creativity* (1998) and *French Global: A New Approach to Literary History* (with Christie McDonald, 2010).

Yale French Studies is the oldest English-language journal in the United States devoted to French and Francophone literature and culture. Each volume is conceived and organized by a guest editor or editors around a particular theme or author. Interdisciplinary approaches are particularly welcome, as are contributions from scholars and writers from around the world. Recent volumes have been devoted to a wide variety of subjects, among them: Levinas; Perec; Paulhan; Haiti; Belgium; Crime Fiction; Surrealism; Material Culture in Medieval and Renaissance France; and French Education.

Yale French Studies is published twice yearly by Yale University Press (yalebooks.com) and may be accessed on JSTOR (jstor.org).

For information on how to submit a proposal for a volume of *Yale French Studies*, visit yale.edu/french and click "Yale French Studies."